ROME

Text by
FILIPPO COARELLI

Foreword by
PIER LUIGI NERVI

MONUMENTS OF CIVILIZATION

ROME

THE READER'S DIGEST ASSOCIATION LIMITED, LONDON

We gratefully acknowledge the courtesy of the Harvard University Press for allowing us to quote excerpts from the following texts, all of which they hold in copyright and which they publish in their *Loeb Classical Library:*

The Attic Nights of Aulus Gellius, translated by
John C. Rolfe. Copyright 1927.
Ammianus Marcellinus, translated by John C. Rolfe.
Copyright 1935.
Scriptores Historiae Augustae, translated by David
Magie. Copyright 1921.
Remains of Old Latin, translated by E. H. Warmington.
Copyright 1967.

We also gratefully acknowledge permission to quote from:

Urbs Roma: A Source Book of Classical Texts on the City and Its Monuments, by Donald R. Dudley. Copyright 1967 by Phaidon Press, London.

Published by

THE READER'S DIGEST ASSOCIATION LIMITED
25 Berkeley Square London WIX 6AB

London   New York   Montreal   Sydney   Cape Town

by arrangement with Cassell & Co Ltd.,
an imprint of
Cassell Ltd.
35 Red Lion Square, London WC1R 4SG
and at Sydney, Auckland, Toronto, Johannesburg
and an affiliate of The Macmillan Company Inc., New York

® READER'S DIGEST is a registered trademark of The Reader's Digest Association Inc., of Pleasantville, New York, U.S.A.

English translation copyright © 1972 by Mondadori, Milano-Kodansha, Tokyo; originally published in Italian under the title *Grandi Monumenti: ROMA* copyright © 1971 by Mondadori, Milano-Kodansha, Tokyo; copyright © 1971 by Kodansha Ltd., Tokyo, for the illustrations; copyright © 1971 by Mondadori, Milano-Kodansha, Tokyo, for the text.

First published in Great Britain 1974
1st edition, 3rd impression 1979
Printed and bound in Italy by Mondadori, Verona

Editorial Director
GIULIANA NANNICINI
American Editorial Supervisor
JOHN BOWMAN

Frontispiece:
Pozzuoli: Amphitheater. Flavian Era

CONTENTS

FOREWORD

Most people have been forced to approach the ancient Romans by one of two routes: by dispassionately written scientific-historical accounts, or by almost mythic traditional versions. Both approaches, however good, provide only glimpses. Finally, though, we have an approach that, by using the many exciting archaeological discoveries in the decorative arts as well as in the more monumental architecture, brings into view the full-bodied realities of the Roman past. Not many works on ancient Rome can offer such a rich, eloquent, and convincing vision as this. The intellectual characteristics of the Romans, the evolution of their esthetic taste, their daily lives — all come alive. And because of the book's totally conceived design, the reader finds parallel comment and clarification in both the photographs and the text. We should indeed be grateful to the author and everyone else involved for providing this most "full-dimensional" approach to the ancient Roman world.

I think it might be said that a characteristic common to all Roman production is the exceptional care and skill applied to every detail, even the smallest. This is to be seen not only in the Romans' architecture but in all their decorative arts as well — mosaics, frescoes, sculpture, or bas-reliefs. There is no mosaic that has not been perfectly realized, no brickwork with rows that are not masterfully uniform, no capital or bas-relief that is not excellently designed and perfectly executed. I think, too, that this characteristic has a special value, a significance that goes beyond the single object. It serves to demonstrate the mentality that must have been common not only to the artists, engineers, and designers of Rome but also to the Roman workmen. To work together with such patient care, as their structures attest they did, they must all not only have loved their work but fully understood its aim and meaning.

To look at the productions of Roman civilization in this fashion is to obtain the vision of a society that loved the beauty resulting from balance and the harmony of forms, a beauty that may be appreciated by everyone. The long, painstaking work involved in perfect execution must have had this very appreciation and evaluation as its just, and ample, reward. The great masonry monuments of Rome reveal not only a splendid daring in their architectural conception, but accurate execution of every element, even those that are secondary. It is unlikely that this would have been possible without the complete understanding of everyone involved — from the original designer down to the least-skilled workman on the job — of the nobility and importance of their endeavors.

How else can we explain masterpieces such as the Colosseum and the Pantheon, the grandiose boundary walls, the bridges and baths, as well as innumerable public and private edifices for which we have indisputable documentation, unless by taking into account the voluntary and intelligent collaboration of masters and workers? For more

Having acquired which glory, Romulus is said first to have auspiciously thought of building a city, and of establishing a government. In regard to the situation of the city, a circumstance which is most carefully to be considered by him, who endeavours to establish a permanent government; he chose it with incredible skill. For neither did he remove to the sea, although it was a very easy thing for him with his forces, to march through the territory of the Rutulians and Aborigines; neither would he build a city at the mouth of the Tiber, to which place the king Ancus led a colony many years after. For he perceived, with an admirable foresight, that maritime situations were not proper for those cities which were founded in the hope of continuance, or with a view to empire. First, because maritime towns were not only exposed to many dangers, but to unseen ones. For the ground over which an expected enemy moves, as well as an unexpected one, announces his approach beforehand by many indications: by sound itself of a peculiarly tumultuous kind. No enemy can make a march, however forced, without our not only knowing him to be there, but even who he is, and whence he comes. But a maritime enemy and a naval force may be before you, ere any one can suspect him to be come. Nor even when he does come, does he carry before him any indication of who he is, or from whence he comes, or even what he wants. Finally by no kind of sign can it be discerned or determined whether he is a friend or an enemy.

In maritime cities, too, a sort of debasing and changeable manners prevail. New languages and new customs are mingled together, and not only productions but manners are imported from abroad; so that nothing remains entire of the pristine institutions. Even they who inhabit those cities are not faithful to their homes, but with capricious inclinations and longings are carried far from them; and although their persons remain, their minds are rambling and wandering abroad. . . .

Who then more inspiredly than Romulus could secure all the maritime conveniences, and avoid all the defects? placing the city on the banks of a perennial river, broadly flowing with an equal course to the sea. By which the city might receive what it wanted from the ocean, and return whatever was superfluous. Receiving by the same channel all things essential to the wants and the refinements of life, not only from the sea, but likewise from the interior. So that it appears to me, he had foreseen this city, at some period, would be the seat and capital of a mighty empire: for a city placed in any other part of Italy would not easily have been able to acquire such a powerful influence.

CICERO: *The Republic* (II: 3-6)

Rome: The Roman Forum seen from the west.

Culture of Latium and Origins of Rome

Legends surrounding the settlement of Rome date back even beyond the traditional date of the city's founding. The arrival of Aeneas in Latium, for instance, was well known as early as the sixth century B.C., as Etruscan statuettes of Aeneas from this period demonstrate, and Virgil also relates in his *Aeneid* the myths of Evander, king of the Arcadians, who settled on the Palatine Hill, and of Hercules, who landed at the Forum Boarium, where the supreme altar, the *Ara Maxima*, of this god lay. It was traditionally the most ancient sanctuary in the city and preceded the Romulean founding.

The date of the historical founding of the city, as given (in the first century B.C.) by the historian Varro, is 753 B.C., which places Rome's settlement within the framework of the Iron Age culture of Latium. This civilization, typical of a marginal environment, and far more provincial than that of the neighboring Etruscans, is now known rather well, from necropolises discovered in Rome itself (in the Roman Forum, and on the Esquiline and Quirinal hills) and in the nearby Alban Hills. Latium's exact chronology is still uncertain, but since the first archaeological studies there has been a differentiation of its culture into two phases, based on the different burial customs employed. The first, perhaps of the ninth and eighth centuries, was characterized by cremation, with the ashes buried in urns shaped like a hut. In the second phase, burial took place in sarcophagi made of tree trunks, and the cultural homogeneity of the preceding period was ruptured by the importation of artisans' products from countries of the eastern Mediterranean, such as Greece and Cyprus.

The latter phase is often called the "easternizing" or "Orientalizing" phase of Latium's culture. The taste for exotic products, Egyptian or Mesopotamian in origin but imported through Phoenecian-Cypriot or Greek-oriental sources, is thought to correspond to a profound change in social structure. In the eighth century urban civilization asserted itself in Italy, through the foundation of Greek colonial settlements in Sicily and southern Italy, and in Rome it appears that the simple egalitarianism of the first Iron Age was transformed into a more complex social structure, characterized primarily by the rise of noble clans.

The economic factors that lie at the basis of this transformation are not easy to identify, but the most probable explanation is an increase in agricultural productivity, linked with an improvement in techniques and implements. On the one hand, this gave rise to a considerable increase in population; on the other, it caused a more marked division of labor. The appearance of groups specializing in different functions

THE MEANING OF POMERIUM

The augurs of the Roman people who wrote books *On the Auspices* have defined the meaning of pomerium in the following terms: "The pomerium is the space within the rural district designated by the augurs along the whole circuit of the city without the walls, marked off by fixed bounds and forming the limit of the city auspices." Now, the most ancient pomerium, which was established by Romulus, was bounded by the foot of the Palatine hill. But that pomerium, as the republic grew, was extended several times and included many lofty hills. Moreover, whoever had increased the domain of the Roman people by land taken from an enemy had the right to enlarge the pomerium.

Therefore it has been, and even now continues to be, inquired why it is that when the other six of the seven hills of the city are within the pomerium, the Aventine alone, which is neither a remote nor an unfrequented district, should be outside the pomerium; and why neither king Servius Tullius nor Sulla, who demanded the honour of extending the pomerium, nor later the deified Julius, when he enlarged the pomerium, included this within the designated limits of the city.

Messala wrote that there seemed to be several reasons for this, but above them all he himself approved one, namely, because on that hill Remus took the auspices with regard to founding the city, but found the birds unpropitious and was less successful in his augury than Romulus. "Therefore," says he, "all those who extended the pomerium excluded that hill, on the ground that it was made ill-omened by inauspicious birds."

AULUS GELLIUS: *Attic Nights* (XIII:14)

THE SACRED BOUNDARY OF ROMULEAN ROME

But I think it not impertinent to show where the first foundations began, and what was the circuit fixed by Romulus. Now, from the Ox Market, where still is seen the brazen statue of a bull, because by that animal the plow is drawn, a furrow was cut to describe the boundaries of the town, so as to include the great altar of Hercules: thence, stones were placed, at certain intervals, along the foot of mount Palatine, to the altar of Consus; soon after, to the Old Courts; then, to the small temple of the Lares; and, lastly, to the great Roman forum, which, as well as the Capitol, it is believed, was added to the city, not by Romulus, but by Tatius. With the increase of her empire, the city afterward continued to increase: and what were the boundaries now established by Claudius is easily learned, as they are detailed in the public records.

TACITUS: *The Annals* (XII:24)

created a need for a centralized power, not only political, but military and religious as well, to unify the different groups.

Once the specialized function of government was recognized, the city-state was born, and the conditions of a homogeneous culture, which was most likely monarchical, were tempered by the rise of a noble oligarchy. Certainly legends of Rome's early history give it kings at this period. The traditional stories of the first four kings — from Romulus, who reputedly founded the city in 753, to Ancus Martius, whose rule reputedly ended in 616 — make it hardly accidental that this period coincides with what archaeologists have called the second phase of Latium culture.

Geographic and Economic Setting

The importance of Rome's location for the later development of the city did not escape the notice of her writers such as Livy and Cicero. The recital of the facts has become a cliché, yet they are extremely important. The city grew up on a group of seven hills facing a ford of the Tiber, the last before its mouth, where a deep bend in the stream produced an excellent natural port, the meeting place of ships coming from the sea and products for export coming from the interior. Here the two most important strategic and commercial routes in central Italy crossed: the water road of the Tiber, and the land road coming from Etruria toward the river ford, beyond which the two major roads to Campania and southern Italy began — one following the Liris river, the future Via Latina, and the other the Pontine valleys, the future Appian Way.

From the beginning, the advantage of this position was clear. The first bridge thrown over the Tiber, according to tradition, was the

Rome: The Tiber near the Isle of the Tiber and the Forum Boarium. (The Isle is visible on the right.) On the left is the Emilian Bridge, now called the Ponte Rotto — the first built in brick, in two phases, 179 and 142 B.C. — of which only one arch remains. The ford of the Tiber was situated here, and the oldest traces of habitation in Rome were discovered in this area, where the most ancient sanctuary in Rome, the Ara Maxima of Hercules, was located, as well as the primitive river port.

REASONS FOR ROME'S GREATNESS

Not without good reason did gods and men select this place for founding a city: these most healthful hills; a commodious river, by means of which the produce of the soil may be conveyed from the inland countries, by which maritime supplies may be obtained; close enough to the sea for all purposes of convenience, and not exposed by too much proximity to the dangers of foreign fleets; a situation in the center of the regions of Italy, singularly adapted by nature for the increase of a city. The very size of so new a city is a proof.

LIVY: *The History of Rome* (V:54)

wooden Sublicius bridge, built during the reign of Ancus Martius, in the second half of the seventh century B.C. The occupation of the Aventine and Janiculum hills is attributed to the same king. Flanking the river, the Aventine on the east and the Janiculum on the west dominated the road that, coming from the northwest, crossed the bridge and then the Murtian valley.

The founding of the colony at Ostia, at the mouth of the Tiber, is also attributed by tradition to Ancus Martius. The seventh century was undoubtedly a period of great and rapid change for Rome, both economic and social, and the greatly increased trade relations with the Near East and Greece obviously contributed to the formation of a new ruling class and a new culture. Poor earthen tombs began to be replaced by grandiose chamber tombs, which indicate the domination of noble clans, and the formation of oligarchical power. The great Etruscan and Latin tombs of Cerveteri (ancient Caere) and Palestrina (whose extraordinary golden tomb furnishings are now the pride of the Villa Giulia Museum in Rome) belong to this Orientalizing phase of central Italian civilization. Although nothing of the same sort has been discovered in Rome itself, due perhaps simply to the destruction caused by the continuity of life there, the fact remains that the city held the key position both for the domination of Latium and for communications between north and south. And a little later, the Etruscans, the most civilized people in early Italy, settled in Rome.

Etruscan Heritage and Formation of Urban Rome

The last three kings of Rome have Etruscan names. Tarquinius Priscus, the first of them (616-578), was said to have come from the

Etruscan city of Tarquinia during the last part of the seventh century B.C., in the reign of Ancus Martius. Under Ancus, Tarquinius so excelled as commander of cavalry, among other things, that upon Ancus Martius' death the Romans chose him as their king.

Although the kings of Rome *are* legendary, legend often tells truths that have real historical value and that other evidence of history and archaeology supports. During the sixth century B.C., in the years corresponding to the traditional reigns of the last three kings, a transformation occurred in Rome that can be related only to a more or less profound "Etruscanization" of the city. Some modern historians have imagined that Etruscan domination of Rome came about through violent conquest, but this is most improbable. There is no mention of it in traditional history, which speaks merely of the peaceful arrival of a family, the Tarquins, who integrate with other citizens and end by taking over power. Etruscans in Rome must always have been a small, if politically dominant, minority, for it is otherwise difficult to explain the persistence of the language, religion, and other fundamental elements of Latin culture, which come through the period of Etruscan domination practically intact. As in the case of the Normans in southern Italy during the medieval period, it seems probable that Etruscan domination was realized through the slow process of infiltration of small groups that, by virtue of their greater technical abilities — not only in the military field, but in political and administrative organization, architecture and the figurative arts, handicrafts, and certain aspects of the divination rites of the haruspices (the Etruscan soothsayers) — end by taking over the principal levers of power.

The qualitative leap taken by Roman civilization after the insertion of the Etruscan element was considerable. The unhealthy valley floor was reclaimed by great works such as the Cloaca Maxima drainage system. Between the Capitoline and the Palatine hills the drained plain was paved, and became the economic and political center of the city, the Forum. The building of sepulchers in this area stopped, and dwellings of wood and brickwork replaced the straw huts. In place of the open-air sanctuaries, the first temples of Etruscan type were built, with rich decorations of polychrome terra-cotta, and anthropomorphic images of the gods, a Greek custom handed down through the Etruscans.

Reforms of Servius Tullius and the Servian Wall

The reign of Tarquinius Priscus' successor, Servius Tullius (578-534) is particularly important in tradition. A remarkable series of reforms is attributed to him, from the centurial disposition of the army and the distribution of the population into territorial "tribes," to the introduction of coins and the creation of numerous cults and sanctuaries. Modern historiography has rejected most of these feats as anachronistic, but a more accurate study of the sources, and important archaeological discoveries, have fairly well established the essential historical truth of the figure and works of Servius Tullius.

Tradition has it that Servius Tullius was the son of a woman slave of king Tarquinius and a divine genius that rose from the flames of her hearth. His supposed divine origin has been used as an argument against his historical authenticity, but the legend of divine birth is obviously propaganda. It was probably used by Servius to justify his assumption of tyrannical power. Cyrus, Alexander, and Julius Caesar were publicized by their own "propaganda bureaus" in similar fashion, yet this is no reason to doubt their historical existence.

The political activity of Servius was perfectly consistent with his obscure origins. According to Etruscan tradition, preserved in a speech given by the Emperor Claudius and by paintings in the Francois Tomb

THE ARRIVAL OF TARQUIN PRISCUS IN ROME

In the reign of Ancus, Lucumo, a rich and enterprising man, came to settle at Rome, prompted chiefly by the desire and hope of obtaining great preferment there, which he had no means of attaining at Tarquinii (for there also he was descended from an alien stock). He was the son of Demaratus, a Corinthian, who, flying his country for sedition, had happened to settle at Tarquinii, and having married a wife there, had two sons by her. Their names were Lucumo and Aruns. Lucumo survived his father, and became heir to all his property.... As the Etrurians despised Lucumo, because sprung from a foreign exile, Tanaquil could not bear the affront, and regardless of the innate love of her native country, provided she might see her husband advanced to honours, she formed the determination to leave Tarquinii. Rome seemed particularly suited for her purpose. In this state, lately founded, where all nobility is recent and the result of merit, there would be room for her husband, a man of courage and activity. Tatius a Sabine had been king of Rome: Numa had been sent for from Cures to reign there: Ancus was sprung from a Sabine mother, and rested his nobility on the single statue of Numa. She easily persuades him, as being ambitious of honours, and one to whom Tarquinii was his country only on the mother's side. Accordingly, removing their effects they set out together for Rome. They happened to have reached the Janiculum; there, as he sat in the chariot with his wife, an eagle, suspended on her wings, gently stooping, takes off his cap, and flying round the chariot with loud screams, as if she had been sent from heaven for the very purpose, orderly replaced it on his head, and then flew aloft. Tanaquil is said to have received this omen with great joy, being a woman well skilled, as the Etrurians generally are, in celestial prodigies, and embracing her husband, bids him hope for high and elevated fortune: that such bird had come from such a quarter of the heavens and the messenger of such a god: that it had exhibited the omen around the highest part of man: that it had lifted the ornament placed on the head of man, to restore it to the same, by direction of the gods. Carrying with them these hopes and thoughts, they entered the city, and having purchased a house there, they gave out the name of Lucius Tarquinius Priscus. His being a stranger and very rich, caused him to be taken notice of by the Romans. He also promoted his own good fortune by his affable address, by the courteousness of his invitations, and by conciliating those whom he could by acts of kindness; until a report of him reached even to the palace; and by paying court to the king with politeness and address, he in a short time so improved the acquaintance to the footing of intimate friendship, that he was present at all public and private deliberations, foreign and domestic; and being now tried in every trust, he was at length, by the king's will, appointed guardian to his children.

LIVY: *The History of Rome* (I:34)

Rome: Head of a helmeted divinity (perhaps Minerva) from the "sacred area" of St. Omobono (circa 540 B.C.). The sanctuaries of Fortuna and of the Mater Matuta, identifiable with those found in this area, are supposed to have been founded by Servius Tullius; in fact the dates of these temple terra-cotta pieces coincide with the traditional dates of his rule. (Antiquario Communale, Rome.)

Rome: A terra-cotta antefix in the shape of a Silenus' head, from the Esquiline. Sixth century B.C. (Antiquario Communale, Rome.)

(an Etruscan tomb found at Vulci) he was an adventurer called Mastarna, the leader of an armed band, and took power in Rome by force. His power, like that of the tyrants in Greece at the same time, was evidently based on the support of the lower classes in the population, which might account for the legend of his slave origin. Above all, however, he had the support of the merchants, artisans, and small and ordinary farm owners. Those against his power, as well as that of all the other Etruscan rulers, were the old patrician groups, the great landowners, who had until that time been the ruling class. In order to break up the force of these factions and their clientele, a transformation of both the social and military structures was necessary.

The pre-Etruscan city of Rome consisted of three noble tribes, a division which was the basis of both the military and the political structure; in archaic societies, the two seem always to be closely connected. Servius divided the city into four tribes on the basis of territory, dissolving the link that bound the state organization to that of the nobles. He then made military service dependent on wealth, with the richest classes those most liable to call-up, a system which had previously been used in Greece. Instead of an army in which each "people" furnished its own contingents, constituting almost a private army, the new system produced a citizen's army, directly dependent on the king — that is, on the state power. Even if this change had not been politically necessary, it would eventually have had to be made for purely military reasons. The development of the hoplite infantry tactics made obsolete the "heroic" army of leaders adept at single combat, followed by an amorphous mass of soldiery. It required instead a large number of warriors armed uniformly and trained to fight in ordered ranks. This military "revolution," which the Etruscans borrowed from the Greeks; went hand in hand with the socio-economic transformations of the period, as the newly rich middle classes claimed their share of power from the older nobility.

Great economic development must have characterized Rome in the sixth century B.C. From economic and strategic points of view, the city lay in a key area, and, as it developed, its links with the other great centers of Etruria must have grown stronger. Some of this growth is reflected in several monuments from this period that have been uncovered. A group of terra-cotta architectural ornaments discovered in the Roman Forum, in the Forum Boarium, on the Capitoline and the Esquiline hills, attest to the existence of numerous temples and chapels as early as the sixth century, confirming what Roman authors say about the founding of sanctuaries by the last three kings.

Building activity seems to have been particularly intense during the reign of Servius Tullius. The erection of the boundary wall of the city is attributed to him, as well as a series of temples, dedicated for the most part to Fortuna, goddess not only of fortune and fate, but embracing functions later assumed by Venus and Juno.

Most authorities have attributed the boundary wall, although called "Servian," to the later, Republican phase of Roman history. The parts now visible, made of tufa stone, can probably be attributed to a period shortly after the conquest of the city by the Gauls under Brennus, in 390 B.C., when the walls were restored (as Livy notes). There may have been a more ancient phase of construction, however. Parts of the wall are made of friable tufa, used for the most part only in the most ancient monuments known. Furthermore, at a certain point on the Aventine Hill, the stone tufa wall of the fourth century is set upon the friable tufa one, older without a doubt. To these archaeological considerations others of a more general historical character can be added. It is hard to believe that Rome in the sixth century did not have some bulwark such as the other Etruscan cities had. The use of the hills as citadels may have been sufficient in earlier periods, when Rome was a collection of small, separate villages, but they were surely not adequate for a united city that included large flat areas absolutely

devoid of natural defense. Servius Tullius is credited with adding to the city the Esquiline, Quirinal and Viminal hills. Unlike the Palatine and the Capitoline hills, these were not isolated heights; they were sprawling features of the landscape, spread out over a large plateau-like area. To secure them for the city, a particularly stout defense on the eastern side of the city was needed, and tradition has it that Servius Tullius built an *agger*, or mound, an elaborate fortification consisting of a wall with a large rampart at the back and a ditch, which brought within the city the plateau between the Quirinal and the Esquiline.

Temples and Artistic Culture of Etruscan Rome

There is also some archaeological proof, though indirect, of Servius Tullius' authenticity. There is proof at any rate of the plausibility of his chronology as handed down by ancient writers. It is related to the sanctuaries, whose history was generally translated with absolute precision. It is known that the holiday of the god was celebrated each year on the day the temple was originally dedicated. There was also a custom of setting a nail in the wall of the temple each year. This was done with the Temple of Jupiter Capitolinus, and it certainly may have been done in other more ancient sanctuaries. Excavations near the church of Saint Omobono, in the area of the ancient Forum Boarium, have brought to light twin temples in which it is possible to identify, on the basis of literary sources that indicated their position, the sanctuaries of Fortuna and the Mater Matuta. According to tradition, these were founded by Servius Tullius. The buildings reveal numerous layers of construction, which go up to the late Imperial Age, but the most ancient remains, only partially explored, have yielded terracotta work that can be dated at the middle of the sixth century B.C. or a little later. The imported Greek ceramics found in this layer also date from the sixth century. The correspondence between the traditional

THE ACTIVITIES OF TARQUIN SUPERBUS ("THE PROUD")

Tarquinius, having thus acquired possession of Gabii, concluded a peace with the nation of the Aequans, renewed the treaty with the Etrurians, and then turned his thoughts to the internal business of the city: among which, the object of his principal concern was to leave the temple of Jupiter, on the Tarpeian mount, a monument of his reign and of his name, to testify, that of two Tarquinii, both of whom reigned, the father had vowed, and the son completed it. . . . Intent on finishing the temple, he sent for workmen from all parts of Etruria, and converted to that use, not only the public money, but the public labour; and although this, which was in itself no small hardship, was added to the toils of military service, yet the people murmured the less, when they considered that they were employing their hands in erecting temples to the gods. They were afterwards obliged to toil at other works, which, though they made less show, were attended with greater difficulty; the erecting seats in the circus, and conducting under ground the principal sewer, the receptacle of all the filth of the city; two works to which the magnificence of modern times can scarcely produce anything equal. After the people had been fatigued by these labours, the king, considered so great a multitude as a burden to the city, where there was not employment for them, and wishing at the same time to extend the frontiers of his dominions, by means of colonies, sent a number of colonists to Signia and Circeii, to serve as barriers to the city, against an enemy, both by land and sea.

LIVY: *The History of Rome* (I:55)

Rome: Peristyle of the House of the Vestal-Virgins in the Forum. From the most ancient times, their quarters lay near the ciruclar Temple of Vesta. Statues of the Chief Vestals were placed along the wall of the portico; some of these are visible in the photograph.

chronology of Servius Tullius, 578-534 B.C., and what can be gathered from archaeological evidence is obvious.

The most notable monument built in Etruscan Rome, however, was the Temple of Jupiter Capitolinus. This temple alone would be sufficient testimony to the level of power and wealth the city attained during the Etruscan period. Conceived and begun under Tarquinius Priscus, the temple was finished during the reign of Tarquinius Superbus. Its inauguration date is known from the ancient calendars and from the list of Roman consuls, and is the first certain chronological reference in Roman history: 509 or 508 B.C. The date coincides with the one

Detail from the statue of Apollo from Veii. End of the sixth century B.C. This image of the god, together with those of others discovered at Veii, was placed on the roof of the temple along its central beam, in the manner of acroteria. The discovery of these magnificent sculptures at the beginning of this century was proof of the existence of an important school of artists in the Etruscan city, probably associated with Vulca of Veii, creator of the terra-cotta ornament for the Temple of Jupiter Capitolinus (509 B.C.). (Villa Giulia Museum, Rome.)

THE SEWERS OF ROME

The public sewers, too, a work more stupendous than any; as mountains had to be pierced for their construction, and, like the hanging city which we recently mentioned, navigation had to be carried on beneath Rome; an event which happened in the aedileship of M. Agrippa, after he had filled the office of consul.

For this purpose, there are seven rivers, made, by artificial channels, to flow beneath the city. Rushing onward, like so many impetuous torrents, they are compelled to carry off and sweep away all the sewerage; and swollen as they are by the vast accession of the pluvial waters, they reverberate against the sides and bottom of their channels. Occasionally, too, the Tiber, overflowing, is thrown backward in its course, and discharges itself by these outlets. . . . and yet, built as they were in the days of Tarquinius Priscus, seven hundred years ago, these constructions have survived, all but unharmed. We must not omit, too, to mention one remarkable circumstance, and all the more remarkable from the fact, that the most celebrated historians have omitted to mention it. Tarquinius Priscus having commenced the sewers, and set the lower classes to work upon them, the laboriousness and prolonged duration of the employment became equally an object of dread to them; and the consequence was, that suicide was a thing of common occurrence, the citizens adopting this method of escaping their troubles. For this evil, however, the king devised a singular remedy, and one that has never been resorted to either before that time or since: for he ordered the bodies of all who had been thus guilty of self-destruction, to be fastened to a cross, and left there as a spectacle to their fellow-citizens and a prey to birds and wild beasts. The result was, that that sense of propriety which so peculiarly attaches itself to the Roman name. . . . It is said that Tarquinius made these sewers of dimensions sufficiently large to admit of a wagon laden with hay passing along them.

PLINY THE ELDER:
Natural History (XXXVI)

traditionally set as the end of the monarchical period and the beginning of the Republic. Ironically, the sanctuary was probably not inaugurated by Tarquinius Superbus, the last king, but by one of the first consuls of the Roman Republic, Horatius Pulvillus. The monument built to glorify the power of the kings through the centuries ended as the symbol of Republican liberty.

The ideological reasons for construction of the temple are clear. Rome must have enjoyed hegemony in Latium in the regal period, competing on an equal basis with the most important Etruscan cities, with success enough to justify the expense of such an edifice. It seems likely as well that the Temple to Diana that Servius built on the Aventine was used as the center of the Latin League, the transfer of whose headquarters to Rome surely indicated the subordination of the League to the Roman state. The Temple of Jupiter — who was worshiped together with Juno and Minerva, the Capitoline trinity and gods of the Roman state cult — was a glorification of the royal power, which was identified with the god on certain occasions, such as a military triumph. This custom remained alive not only for the entire Republican period but on into the Imperial Age.

The dimensions of the temple, whose base is still visible (in the Capitoline Museum) were exceptionally large. Measuring approximately 213 feet by 193 feet, it was the largest Etruscan temple known, with six columns in front and six on the sides, and three chambers for the statues of the three divinities. Like all archaic Etruscan temples, it was built almost entirely of wood — although the podium was made of tufa blocks — and covered with terra-cotta ornaments. The terra-cotta statues for worship, and the rich polychrome terra-cotta decoration, were entrusted to Etruscan artists. The name of one is known, probably the master who directed the work: Vulca of Veii. He made not only the statue of Jupiter but also one of Hercules, which may have been placed in the sanctuary of the *Ara Maxima*. The sculptures were made at Veii, or so Pliny asserts in talking of the great chariot that was placed on the roof of the edifice as an acroterium.

In the course of time, all these sculptures have been destroyed; the temple passed through many fires and renovations. It is still possible to gather a precise idea of what they looked like, however. Excavations at Veii have revealed the remains of a temple built at the same time as the Temple of Jupiter Capitolinus. This too was decorated with grandiose terra-cotta sculptures (which are now among the treasures of Rome's Villa Giulia Museum). They reveal the hand of a master who, within the stylistic framework of archaic Etruscan art, influenced by the work of Ionian Greece, achieves a remarkably personal expression, less mannered and more solid than his Ionian models. Vulca's name was mentioned when the discovery was made, and even if the work cannot be assigned to him with absolute certainty, the coincidence of chronology and artistic style make it probable that he was the artist. This is the only case where an Etruscan work can be attributed with any probability to an artist whose name is known.

The celebrated Capitoline She-Wolf, an Etruscan work from the end of the sixth or perhaps the beginning of the fifth century, also shows many of the stylistic qualities of Vulca's work. As is the case with the Apollo of Veii, abstract, archaic Greek elements — for instance, the stylized curls that make up horses' manes and tails — are used, but they are integrated into a simple, organic work of great plastic power. These two masterpieces alone clearly indicate the high artistic level reached in Rome under the Etruscan kings.

In the light of what is presently known of the sixth century in Rome, it is possible to call the period completely historical. The idea of an archaic Rome that, while rubbing elbows with Greeks and Etruscans (to whom Romans owed their alphabet), lingered on in prehistoric mists in the center of that fully evolved and vigorous environment, must be definitively rejected. Far from being isolated and provincial, the "great Rome of the Tarquins" was a full participant in the eco-

nomic, cultural and artistic development of the Greek-influenced Mediterranean world. Rome was even able to make an independent move toward new forms of social and constitutional organization. The rapid formation and growth of a complex, fully articulated urban structure took place in this period, with an economy based not only on forms of pastoral and agricultural exploitation, but on expanding commerce and trade and their related activities. The cultural development of the same time, although probably limited to the elite of the Etruscan or Etruscanized ruling classes, was nonetheless impressive. The ever-growing urbanization, the appearance of buildings used to fulfill new and complex functions, indicates clearly that although Rome may have been founded in 753, in the midst of the Iron Age in Latium, it was through the events of the sixth century that Rome as a city was truly born anew.

Rome: Head of the Capitoline She-Wolf. Beginning of the fifth century B.C. This imposing bronze, the most outstanding in archaic Etruscan art, is of great importance as a document of the activity of Etruscan artists in Rome. Figures of the suckling twins, Romulus and Remus, were added in the sixteenth century A.D. but it is not certain that similar figures were part of the original. (Palazzo dei Conservatori, Rome.)

FORMATION OF ROMAN CULTURE
Republican Period (509-31 B.C.)

Beginnings of the Roman Republic

Exactly what political consequences the fall of the monarchy in Rome had are not clear. Some scholars have interpreted the ouster of the kings as the end of Etruscan domination in the city, but a broad affirmation of this kind contains some ambiguities that must be clarified, for Etruscan domination in Rome was really more cultural than political, anyway. Although an Etruscan League existed, each city within it was absolutely independent. Individual cities could, and often did, make their own alliances and set their own policies, Rome no more or less than the others. So the fall of the Tarquins seems to indicate a constitutional crisis rather than a break in the relationship with Etruria. In other Etruscan cities in the same period a similar phenomenon occurred; they passed from monarchical to republican governments, for the most part through "tyrannical" regimes on the Greek model. It is even likely that some Etruscan families collaborated in the overthrow of the Tarquins in Rome. Collatinus Tarquinius, together with Brutus, was one of the leaders of the revolution, and the consular lists, the *Fasti*, contain Etruscan names as late as 448 B.C. According to some scholars, this proves that the monarchy disappeared only in the second quarter of the fifth century, between 475 and 450. There is no need, however, to equate the existence of the monarchy with the presence of the Etruscans in Rome. The decline of Etruscan power in Campania took place only after their defeat at the hands of the Greeks at Cumae in 474 B.C.; this date corresponds fairly well with the disappearance of Etruscan elements from the Roman consular lists.

Artistic culture in Rome at the beginning of the fifth century certainly shows no major signs of a break with that which prevailed at the end of the sixth century. Relations with Magna Graecia were intensified, however, perhaps as an anti-patrician move. The struggles between patricians and plebeians began at this period, and were to continue to play a major role in the first centuries of the Republic. It is therefore probably no accident that decoration of the Temple of Ceres (Bacchus), Liber and Libera (Proserpine), (gods corresponding to the Greek Demeter, Dionysus and Kore) were entrusted to two Greek artists, Damophilos and Gorgasos. These gods were patrons of agriculture and hence of the wheat trade. Their temple, erected in 496 B.C. at the foot of the Aventine, soon became a stronghold of the plebeians. Varro indicates it was the first edifice in the Greek style erected in Rome. All the previous temples had been built in Etruscan style. The temple of Diana founded by Servius Tullius, placed as it was near the river port, also was favored by the plebeians.

In the course of the fifth century, the temple of Ceres became the distribution center for the grain imported from Etruria and even from Sicily, at the insistence of the plebeian tribunes. The supply of grain to the plebeians, first at half-price and later free, was a revolutionary

THE DECORATION OF THE TEMPLE OF CERES

The most celebrated sculptors were Damophilus and Gorgasus, who were painters as well. These artists adorned with their works, in both kinds, the Temple of Ceres, in the Circus Maximus at Rome; with an inscription in Greek, which stated that the decorations on the right-hand were the workmanship of Damophilus, and those on the left, of Gorgasus. Varro says that, before the construction of this temple, everything was Tuscan in the temples; and that, when the temple was afterwards repaired, the painted coatings of the walls were cut away in tablets and enclosed in frames, but that the figures on the pediments were dispersed.

PLINY THE ELDER:
Natural History (XXXV)

Rome: Temple of Castor and Pollux in the Forum. The three columns still standing belong to a restoration of the Augustan Age. The primitive Temple was dedicated in 484 B.C., in the place where the Dioscuri were supposed to have appeared to announce Rome's victory at Lake Regillus over the Latin League.

political step, and constituted a heated issue between the patricians and the plebeians up to the end of the Republican Age. The agrarian reforms periodically proposed by the revolutionary tribunes, such as the Gracchi, were another.

If there is little political or institutional continuity between the sixth and the first decades of the fifth century, there is economic and cultural continuity, and it can be followed fairly well through the importation of Greek vases, by this time almost exclusively Attic in style. This importation continued uninterrupted up to the middle of the fifth century, although it diminished somewhat in scale. There seems to have been a crisis at mid-century, however. Importation of vases stopped and there was no further introduction of Greek forms of worship. After the temple of Ceres, no more Greek divinities were imported until 433 B.C., when a Temple of Apollo was built in the Campus Martius.

Contrary to what occurred in Greece in the fifth century, Italy in the same period passed through a period of economic and cultural decadence and confusion, which began with the destruction of Sybaris in 510 B.C. The great Greek city of Lucania, one of the key trading points between Italy and the eastern Mediterranean, was destroyed by its rival, Croton. Then, after their defeat at Cumae, the Etruscans went through a political and economic recession. Although the Greeks were the victors for the moment, in the last years of the century they experienced a crisis as well, for the Carthaginians occupied and destroyed almost all the towns of Greek Sicily at that time, except for Syracuse and a few others, and the Italic populations in the interior moved toward the coasts of southern Italy and Sicily to occupy, one by one, the Greek cities there. Only Tarentum and Naples were able to offer resistance and remain Greek.

The Italic Community

The intensity of trade and economic relations in the sixth century was matched by an exceptional cultural flowering, in which Etruria and Rome participated on the same level as the cities of Magna Graecia; but the fifth century was a period of decline and closure, of fragmentation and provincialization of culture. Roman culture of this period is little known, partly because of this. It seems to have been a period of heroic endurance, of universal and daily struggles against the Sabines, the Etruscans, and the Volscians. Hints of this are found in the writing of Livy.

The fourth century, however, was an age of vigorous renewal on all levels. The fusion of the indigenous population and the Greeks in southern Italy and Sicily gave rise to an extremely florid and mixed civilization, less brilliant but all in all more robust than that of the sixth century which had been based on the power of an elite and was not deeply rooted. In 396 B.C., Rome ended its mortal duel with the Etruscan city of Veii by destroying it, and recovered from the violent shock of the sack of Rome by the Gauls in 390. The Romans craved wider influence, in the north toward Etruria and in the south toward Campania and the cities of Magna Graecia, but it was necessary first for them to overcome the Samnites, the powerful confederation of peoples who dominated the territory (corresponding to present-day Molise) east and south of Rome. The natural area expansion for the Samnites, too, was Campania.

The general economic revival quickly led to more intense relations of every kind, and little by little a unified Greek-speaking cultural community was formed. It extended from Etruria to Sicily, with its extreme points at Capua, Tarentum, Syracuse, and the outlying Etruscan cities. Pottery was no longer imported from Athens, but made locally. Its style, though derived from Greece, displays a new

A TREATY BETWEEN ROME AND CARTHAGE (509 B.C.)

"Between the Romans and their allies and the Carthaginians and their allies there shall be peace and alliance upon these conditions. Neither the Romans nor their allies shall sail beyond the Fair Promontory, unless compelled by bad weather or an enemy. And in case that they are forced beyond it, they shall not be allowed to take or purchase any thing, except what is barely necessary for refitting their vessels, or for sacrifice; and they shall depart within five days. The merchants, that shall offer any goods to sale in Sardinia, or any part of Afric, shall pay no customs, but only the usual fees to the scribe and crier; and the public faith shall be a security to the merchant, for whatever he shall sell in the presence of these officers. If any of the Romans land in that part of Sicily which belongs to the Carthaginians, they shall suffer no wrong or violence in any thing. The Carthaginians shall not offer any injury to the Ardeates, Antiates, Laurentines, Circaeans, Tarracinians, or any other people of the Latins, that have submitted to the Roman jurisdiction. Nor shall they possess themselves of any city of the Latins that is not subject to the Romans. If any one of these be taken, it shall be delivered to the Romans in its entire state. The Carthaginians shall not build any fortress in the Latin territory: and if they land there in a hostile manner they shall depart before night."

POLYBIUS: *History* (III:3)

RECONSTRUCTION OF ROME AFTER THE GALLIC FIRE (390 B.C.)

The law [under discussion] being rejected, the building of the city commenced in several parts at once. Tiles were supplied at the public expense. The privilege of hewing stone and felling timber wherever each person wished was granted, security being taken that they would finish the buildings on that year. Their haste took away all attention to the regulating course of the streets, whilst, setting aside all distinction of property, they build on any part that was vacant. That is the reason why the ancient sewers, at first conducted through the public streets, now in many places pass under private houses, and why the form of the city appears more like one taken up by individuals, than regularly portioned out [by commissioners].

LIVY: *The History of Rome* (V:55)

Scipio Barbatus

Lucius Cornelius Scipio Long-beard, Gnaeus' begotten son, a valiant gentleman and wise, whose fine form matched his bravery surpassing well, was aedile, consul and censor among you; he took Taurasia and Cisauna, in fact Samnium; he overcame all the Lucanian land and brought hostages therefrom.

Lucius, Son of Barbatus

This man Lucius Scipio, as most agree, was the very best of all good men at Rome. A son of Long-beard, he was aedile, consul and censor among you; he it was who captured Corsica, Aleria too, a city. To the Goddesses of Weather he gave deservedly a temple.

Publius Cornelius, Son of Africanus

You who have worn the honoured cap of Jupiter's holy priest: Death caused all your virtues, your honour, good report and valiance, your glory and your talents to be short-lived. If you had but been allowed long life in which to enjoy them, an easy thing it would have been for you to surpass by great deeds the glory of your ancestors. Wherefore, O Publius Cornelius Scipio, begotten son of Publius, joyfully does Earth take you to her bosom.

Lucius, Son of Hispallus

Great virtues and great wisdom holds this stone
With tender age. Whose life but not his honour
Fell short of honours; he that lieth here
Was ne'er outdone in virtue; twenty years
Of age to burial-places was he entrusted.
This, lest ye ask why honours none to him
        Were e'er entrusted.

Gnaes Scipio Hispanus

Gnaeus Cornelius Scipio Hispanus, son of Gnaeus, praetor, curule aedile, quaestor, tribune of soldiers (twice); member of the Board of Ten for Judging Law-suits; member of the Board of Ten for Making Sacrifices.

By my good conduct I heaped virtues on the virtues of my clan; I begat a family and sought to equal the exploits of my father. I upheld the praise of my ancestors, so that they are glad that I was created of their line. My honours have ennobled my stock.

Tombs of the Scipios

result was the total ruin of the class. The farmers went into debt to survive, but unable to meet their obligations, they forfeited their possessions to a small number of families who had become enormously rich through war booty and the administration of the provinces and newly captured areas. The large landed estates that resulted were given over to a system of operation involving slave labor, plentiful after the wars of conquest, while the class of small landowners disappeared. The powerful families who had created the estates took over political power in Rome, which was henceforth governed oligarchically. There was no further identification between the citizen-landowner and the soldier, and little by little the army became a specialized function within the state, completely cut off from civil society. At the end of the second century, the demagogue Marius was to reap the harvest of this process by transforming the army finally into a professional group, personally bound to its leader rather than to the state.

The economic crisis was particularly grave in Magna Graecia and southern Etruria, exactly in those areas that in the preceding centuries had been the cultural centers. Cities like Croton, Locri, Metapontum, Tarquinia and Cerveteri (Caere) practically disappeared. The treatment given to Tarentum after its conquest by the Romans during the second Punic war is indicative. After a long and cruel siege, the city, which had sided with Carthage against Rome, was taken in 209. It was sacked, much of the population was killed, and thirty thousand citizens were sold into slavery. From a city which had been the most important center for the spread of Hellenism in Italy, Tarentum became practically a provincial village that never again revived.

Recent archaeological investigations confirm this crisis. Around Metaponto, land has been discovered that was subdivided into regular lots, or holdings — "centurization" was the Roman term — as early as the sixth century B.C. The farms that have been excavated show signs of continuous occupation from this period up to the end of the third century B.C., when all the holdings were abandoned. The date coincides with that of the second Punic war. Such a phenomenon in

the ancient world, where the chief form of economy was always the cultivation of land, is a sure indication of economic and cultural collapse. Magna Graecia simply ceased to exist as a civilized society. The Romans attempted to repopulate these areas. Colonies were founded in Sybaris and Tarentum, but with poor results. Instead the large estates, called *latifundia*, worked by formations of slaves or used for large-scale stock-raising, covered vast areas of Magna Graecia, Sicily, and Etruria from the second century forward. The slaves, uprooted from their diverse homelands and condemned to an economy of sheer subsistence, have left hardly any "cultural" traces of their existence, if we exclude the blood memory of the desperate slave wars that shook Magna Graecia and Sicily during the last two centuries of the Republic. Ancient historiography was completely in the hands of the ruling class, and it has left only a pale record of this world, which nevertheless was the economic backbone of the Roman Empire. If written history gives only a glimpse of this world, art history gives no view at all. Negative traces can be found at Rome, however, for the slave system had a tremendous effect on the structure of Roman society, and in turn affected artistic production.

Hellenistic Influx

The essentially homogenous Roman-Italic society of the fourth and third centuries was replaced after the conquests by a profoundly divided one, in which an immense, landless, urban proletariat and a professional army, ideal material for the manipulation of every kind of professional adventurer, were ruled by a few dominant families. The cultural models of a military-agricultural society, which had served up to this time, were in no way suited to the new ruling class, controlling as it did the levers of a gigantic empire. Both on a philosophical level, as a justification of power, and on an artistic level, new cultural models existed in the monarchical states of the Hellenistic world: Macedonia, Egypt, and Syria. A mere imitation of them was impossible, however, since the Hellenistic adherence to a concept of absolute monarchy — where kings, from Alexander on, took on the aspect of religious heads as well, to the point of being deified while still alive — was impossible in the context of Roman traditionalism. Attempts of this kind were made in Rome, but they were almost always timid and circumspect. Julius Caesar paid for his daring innovations with his life. For the Romans, every revolution had to assume the aspect of a return to the customs of their ancestors.

The culture that formed in Rome in Hellenizing circles such as that of the Scipio family during the course of the second century, then, was neither a simple continuation of Greek culture in a different environment nor an imitation. The Romans were really too shrewd to accept a foreign tradition uncritically, even if they knew it to be superior in some ways to their own. The choice of elements from foreign culture had to be functional. After an initial phil-Hellenic enthusiasm, there was a period of reflection and reaction. Cato the Censor was the major adversary of indiscriminate Hellenization, and more is to be seen in his writings on the subject than reactionary envy and malice. He was no fool, and he knew Greek culture quite well, though he preferred, as did Cicero later on, to give the opposite impression. Cato and others acted as filters and set criteria of choice for the Romans. In 150 B.C., when the Greek philosopher Carneades, in a speech on justice, dared to question the right of Roman imperialism, he was immediately expelled from Rome. Yet approval, protection, and praise were given Panaetius of Rhodes, who adapted Stoicism to the needs of Roman society; it became the official philosophy of the Roman ruling class.

Rome: Seated female figure in terra cotta, part of a pediment decoration discovered in Via San Gregorio in Rome. Circa 130 B.C. (Capitoline Museums, Rome).

Rome: This circular temple of marble, near the Tiber (perhaps of Hercules Victor), is the work of a Greek architect working in Rome at the end of the second century B.C.

Following page:

Above:
Rome: Relief from a Republican Age trophy, originally on the Capitol. Second to first century B.C. From the left, a cuirass with decorations in the form of heads of Medusa and Victory; then, between two trophies, a round shield with a profile of Minerva's head. The work of a Hellenistic artist, possibly an Egyptian, as the quality of the material would seem to indicate. (Capitoline Museums, Rome.)

Below:
Rome: Fragment of a monumental sepulcher with the representation of a historic scene. 40-30 B.C. (Capitoline Museums, Rome.)

The people erected scaffolds in the forum, in the circuses, as they call their buildings for horse-races, and in all other parts of the city where they could best behold the show. The spectators were clad in white garments; all the temples were open, and full of garlands and perfumes; the ways were cleared and kept open by numerous officers, who drove back all who crowded into or ran across the main avenue. This triumph lasted three days. On the first, which was scarcely long enough for the sight, were to be seen the statues, pictures, and colossal images which were taken from the enemy, drawn upon two hundred and fifty chariots. On the second was carried in a great many waggons the finest and richest armour of the Macedonians, both of brass and steel, all newly polished and glittering; the pieces of which were piled up and arranged purposely with the greatest art, so as to seem to be tumbled in heaps carelessly and by chance: helmets were thrown upon shields, coats of mail upon greaves; Cretan targets, and Thracian bucklers and quivers of arrows, lay huddled amongst horses' bits, and through these there appeared the points of naked swords, intermixed with long Macedonian sarissas. All these arms were fastened together with just so much looseness that they struck against one another as they were drawn along, and made a harsh and alarming noise, so that, even as spoils of a conquered enemy, they could not be beheld without dread. After these waggons loaded with armour there followed three thousand men who carried the silver that was coined, in seven hundred and fifty vessels, each of which weighed three talents, and was carried by four men. Others brought silver bowls and goblets and cups, all disposed in such order as to make the best show, and all curious as well for their size as the solidity of their embossed work.

On the third day, early in the morning, first came the trumpeters, who did not sound as they were wont in a procession or solemn entry, but such a charge as the Romans use when they encourage the soldiers to fight. Next followed young men wearing frocks with ornamented borders, who led to the sacrifice a hundred and twenty stalled oxen, with their horns gilded, and their heads adorned with ribbons and garlands; and with these were boys that carried basins for libation, of silver and gold. After this was brought the gold coin, which was divided into vessels that weighed three talents, like those that contained the silver; they were in number seventy-seven. These were followed by those that brought the consecrated bowl which Aemilius had caused to be made, that weighed ten talents, and was set with precious stones. Then were exposed to view the cups of Antigonus and Seleucus, and those of the Thericlean make, and all the gold plate that was used at Perseus's table. Next to these came Perseus's chariot, in which his armour was placed, and on that his diadem. And, after a little intermission, the king's children were led captives, and with them a train of their attendants, masters, and teachers, all shedding tears, and stretching out hands to the spectators, and making the children themselves also beg and entreat their compassion.

PLUTARCH: *The Life of Aemilius Paulus* (32-3)

An operation of the same kind took place in the arts, There was no careless and indiscriminate introduction of Hellenistic art, but once again a choice. Original works of Greek art, rather than their Italic derivations, reached Rome in the wake of the wars against the Carthaginians and the Hellenistic kingdoms. The conquest of Syracuse in 211 and Tarentum in 209 began the sack of art works that little by little brought together in Rome a large part of Greek artistic production, from the Archaic to the Hellenistic periods. At the same time, interest in works of art among the cultured in Rome was increased by the presence there of Greek artists and writers. After an initial period of enchantment, however, Roman practicality prevailed; the advantages of the new situation were esteemed, but their dangers were seen as well.

Aspects of Hellenistic tradition that were difficult to integrate were rejected. They were sometimes accepted on the private level, but in the public and ceremonial art of Rome — large-scale architecture, images for cult worship, the painting and sculpture dealing with historical subjects — a more radical choice was made. The classical canons of neo-Attic art, inspired by the great Greek works of the fourth and fifth centuries B.C., were adopted, rather than the Hellenistic. They were thought to be more suited to the culture of a centralizing and aristocratic elite such as had risen out of the new political and social situation in Rome.

The situation deserves at least a summary. It was in the look and life of Rome itself at this time that the radical political and economic split could be most clearly seen. There was naturally a struggle among the dominant families for the approbation of the large urban proletariat created by the impoverishment of Italy. Flocking to Rome in numbers, the landless farmers created an enormous urban problem, and immense, poverty-stricken neighborhoods grew up. As a means to counter these, "rival projects" were endowed and elaborate areas of public resort were built — such as that around the Circus Flaminius in the Campus Martius, where Greek sculptors, painters, and architects were employed to build sanctuaries, gardens, and porticoes. The circular temple in the Forum Boarium, most likely a Temple of Hercules, is a particularly remarkable example. It has recently been recognized as the work of a Greek architect of the second century B.C., probably Hermodorus of Salamis, a Greek who worked in Rome at this time, building two temples and the Rome naval base, all in the Campus Martius, between 146 and 102. The sculptors active in Rome during the same period were for the most part Attic (although there was no lack of Rhodians): Timarchides (active around 179), his sons Polycles and Dionysus, and last of all Skopas junior, whose activity extended through the beginning of the first century B.C.

The school or shop of Skopas should possibly be given credit for the first historical relief known in Rome, the so-called Ara of Domitius Enobarbus (today shared by the Louvre and Munich museums). It depicts a retinue of marine divinities and a *lustrum*, the solemn ceremony of purification that marked the end of the quinquennial census. This monument probably formed the base of the statues of Neptune and Amphitrite in the Temple of Neptune, which was built between the Circus Flaminius and the naval base. It is interesting that the first historical relief, a type of monument considered typically Roman, should be the work of a neo-Attic artist. As a matter of fact the sole known precedent in Greece for the work is the sculpted pillar dedicated at Delphi to the glory of L. Emilius Paulus after his victory at Pydna over Perseus, the King of Macedonia, and is thus another work of art by a Greek for a Roman buyer. These works of art, then, were conditioned not so much by the nationality and cultural formation of the artist as by the needs and desires of the buyer. Although executed by Greek artists, these works are at least potentially works of Roman art. It is true that in them Roman content and Greek form are

mechanically combined; they do not blend. A formally original Roman art arrived only after a certain amount of time had passed. In this sense the second century is still a formative period. The decisive moment coincided with the beginning of the first century B.C., the Sullan Age.

Temple of Fortuna at Praeneste

Similar conclusions can be drawn about the great sanctuaries in Latium that were built in this period, renewing the ancient cults in lovely architectural forms: the temple of Fortuna Primigenia at Praeneste, (present-day Palestrina), of Hercules Victor at Tivoli, and of Jupiter Anxur at Terracina. The most remarkable and best preserved of these is that at Palestrina and it is a key example for any understanding and evaluation of the phenomenon of Hellenistic influence. Gigantic in size, the edifice covers an entire hillside of present-day Palestrina. Its series of overlaid stairways, ramps, and terraces end at the top in a large colonnaded area open on the side towards the plain. This colonnaded area is dominated in turn by a semicircular theater area and by the temple proper. The medieval city that occupied a large part of the building was destroyed in the last war, freeing the historic complex for restoration.

Scholars have proposed two different dates for the building: the middle of the second century or the years following Sulla's destruction of Palestrina in 82 B.C. Recently the inclination among experts has been to accept a date sometime in the last quarter of the second century, between 125 and 100. The oldest known, then, of this particular class of monuments, the temple at Palestrina, can be seen as a

Palestrina (ancient Praeneste): The temple of Fortuna Primigenia. This grandiose complex, dating from the last quarter of the second century B.C., occupies, with its terraces, a large part of the hill that overlooks present-day Palestrina.

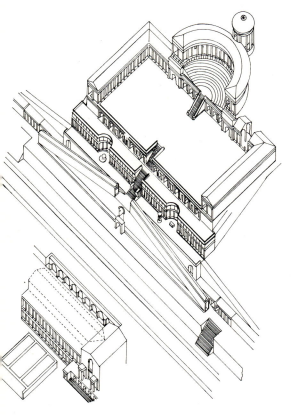

Palestrina (ancient Praeneste): Axonometric plan of the Temple of Fortuna Primigenia (130-110 B.C.).

prototype. Placing and defining the monument is a complex problem, however. Is it Roman or Hellenistic architecture? Such questions can hardly be given clear-cut answers in a historical period that witnesses the meeting of the Roman-Italic and Greek-Hellenistic cultures.

It is obvious that Praeneste would have been inconceivable without Hellenistic architecture, especially that of Asia Minor and the Aegean islands. There are no precedents for it either in an Italic setting or in Magna Graecia. These forms of architecture appear in Latium practically from nowhere, fully mature. In the light of what is known of the history of this period, to speak of originality or novelty would be rather foolish.

Precedents are to be found at Pergamon, and above all at Cos in the sanctuary of Aesculapius and in the arrangement of the acropolis of Lindos in Rhodes. The temple at Palestrina is different from these, but only because it is a logical development of them. Axiality — the vision centered on a median view, with symmetrical lateral elements — has sometimes been seen as a constant of Italic art and spirit, but it is also present in the Hellenistic examples, particularly the acropolis at Lindos. The real novelty at Praeneste is in its technique of construction. Extensive use is made of the vault cast in concrete. It must be admitted that at Praeneste it was employed for practical economic reasons. Such use could be called degenerate; the vault elements were originally hidden by applied architraves, horizontal cornices, and colonnaded porticoes, all traditional elements of Greek architecture.

It was only somewhat later that the esthetic possibilities of vaulting were recognized and appreciated. When this occurred, vaults were not only displayed, they were emphasized. The same process has occurred many times in the history of architecture (the history of the use of reinforced concrete in modern architecture being a good example).

Pompeii: A food storehouse. The products were placed in large terra-cotta jars buried in the earth.

first of all) were always met with fierce opposition: Epicurean philosophy, certain types of spectacle, private luxury. The public aspects of Hellenistic culture were accepted as such more easily than the private aspects. The private aspects eventually penetrated, too, but in Roman culture there always remained a kind of guilty conscience. It seemed impossible to admit in public what one did in private. This curious duplicity is seen even in Cicero. In his famous orations against Verres, when he had to refer to the Greek sculptor Polycletus, one of whose statues had been stolen by the corrupt governor of Sicily, he pretended he had forgotten the sculptor's name and asked his secretary to tell him. "Who? Oh yes, . . . a certain Polycletus." Cicero's letters to Atticus, written at about the same time as his orations were delivered, reveal him to be a most refined connoisseur of Greek art. He asks his distant friend to send him some statues to decorate his Villa Tusculanum, and trembles with expectation, so anxious is he to contemplate them. Even during the Imperial Age, when luxury had already reached a level rarely realized in other civilizations, one of the richest persons in the imperial court, the philosopher Seneca, lost no time in praising

the frugality and poverty of the ancient Romans and citing their habits as good examples.

Again, though, a distinction must be made. Being practical, the Romans had nothing against wealth per se. The peasant avariciousness of the Roman was quite different, however, from the open and enterprising mentality typical of commercial peoples such as the Greeks or the Carthaginians. The essential thing for the Roman, was to maintain a sober and patriarchal style of life and not to abandon himself to vulgar displays of wealth or to rash spending. So it was a problem of form more than of substance. For a Roman of the Republic it was perfectly moral to exploit the Greeks, to use slaves as beasts of burden with the least expense and the greatest profit and then get rid of them when they became old or ill (the example comes from Cato's treatise on agriculture, that mirror of every Roman virtue). It was, however, immoral and reprehensible to use silver at table, dress in the Greek fashion, or speak of useless and dangerous things such as art and philosophy.

While Greek art and techniques established themselves rapidly in the public sphere, their penetration of private life was much slower and later in developing. The higher the social level and the greater the political importance of the persons involved, the slower the penetration. While in Campania, houses and villas of high artistic worth were to be found as early as the middle of the second century, there was nothing similar in Rome until the end of the century. The villa of Scipio Africanus at Literno was described by Seneca as a kind of gloomy fort, with a small and obscure bath in which a Roman of the Imperial Age would have refused to wash. The sepulcher of the Scipio family, who dominated Roman politics in the second century and were considered kings outside their country, astonishes by its poverty and simplicity. The contemporary monumental tombs of Etruria, belonging to persons who would have been happy to be counted among the Scipios' clients, were much richer. In 155 B.C. Scipio Nasica ordered the destruction of a brick theater being built by the censors at the foot of the Palatine, and prohibited the erection of theaters less than a mile from the city. At the same time, almost every little city in Italy had its own brick theater.

By the end of the second century B.C., however, and above all during the first, private life became as completely and sumptuously Hellenistic as public life had already become. Some traces of the old mentality remained, but most were of the sort described above in connection with Seneca and Cicero.

Development of the Hellenistic-Roman House

The same simplicity noted in the Scipios' tomb was to characterize the houses of noble Romans for the greater part of the second century. But from that time on, a new type of house was introduced, the result of the fusion of the ancient Italic dwelling, with its atrium, and the Hellenistic house with its peristyle. (The atrium was an inner court, roofed at the edges but with the center open to the sky; the peristyle is a colonnade surrounding an open court.) As for the decoration of the interior, the so-called First Style, which consisted of stucco painted to imitate walls made of regular, square blocks, must have prevailed even in Rome. In Rome no well-preserved houses of the second century B.C. have yet been discovered. The best examples are to be found in the Campanian cities destroyed by Vesuvius, Pompeii and Herculaneum. It is unlikely that there existed in Rome houses as elaborate as the "House of the Faun," not because of any supposed priority Campania had over Rome (Campania in the first century was in fact economically and culturally a part of the Eternal City). Rather, ideological motives prevented the Roman ruling class from exagger-

THE VILLA OF SCIPIO AFRICANUS AND ITS BATH

I write this to you, Lucilius, from the famous villa of Scipio Africanus, having first paid my devotions to his memory at the altar which I take to be the sepulcher of that great man ...I found this his villa built of square stone, and a wood enclosed with a wall; a turret on each side of the front, by way of bulwark; a large reservoir under the buildings and green walks, sufficient to supply with water a whole army; a bath narrow and somewhat dark after the ancient custom; for our ancestors thought it could not be warm enough unless it was close.

It was therefore a great pleasure to me to reflect upon the custom and manners of Scipio compared with our own. In this little nook was that great man (the dread of Carthage, and to whom Rome was indebted for having once taken it) used to bathe his body when fatigued with rustic labours. For he daily exercised himself in husbandry, and tilled the ground with his own hands, as was customary among our forefathers. Under this low and sordid roof stood Scipio. He disdained not to tread so vile and mean a floor. But who is there in our time that would condescend to bathe in like manner? A man thinks himself poor and mean unless the walls are decorated with large and precious embossments. . . .

SENECA: *Letter to Lucilius* (86)

A CONFLICT BETWEEN THE NUCERIANS AND POMPEIANS IN THE AMPHITHEATER AT POMPEII (A.D. 59)

About the same time, a trivial altercation gave rise to a sanguinary conflict between the inhabitants of the colonies of Nuceria and Pompeii, at the celebration of a combat of gladiators exhibited by Livineius Regulus, whose expulsion from the senate I have before recounted. For, as they rallied each other with the freedom usual among the inhabitants of small towns, they proceeded to abuse, then to throwing stones, and at length they had recourse to arms: but the people of Pompeii, where the spectacle was exhibited, were too strong for their opponents. In consequence, numbers of the Nucerians were conveyed to Rome, wounded and mutilated; and many bewailed the death of sons and fathers. The cognizance of this affair was by the prince left to the senate, and by them to the consuls; and on their report of the merits of the case to the fathers, the people of Pompeii were prohibited from holding any such public meeting for ten years, and the societies they had instituted contrary to the laws were dissolved.

TACITUS: *The Annals* (XIV:17)

Herculaneum: House of the Wooden Partition, the atrium. One of the most famous houses of the Republican Age, it was restored during the Imperial Age, and increased in height. The basin of the impluvium at the center shows the two phases of construction.

The Mosaic of Alexander, from the House of the Faun in Pompeii. Second century B.C. This is the most important and elaborate mosaic of the Hellenistic period known. Almost certainly executed by Greek artists, probably from Alexandria, it may have been imported already complete, rather

than executed on the spot. Like all mosaics of the period, it takes its inspiration from a great painting, perhaps the work of Philoxenes of Eretria, depicting one of the battles between Alexander and Darius (either at Issus or Gaugamela). (Naples National Museum).

ated private luxury, whereas the same motives posed no obstacles for Campanian aristocrats, landowners, and merchants.

The Hellenistic-Roman dwelling with its elegant architectural forms, ornamental paintings, sculptures, and gardens, was one of the most refined products of ancient civilization. Its sudden appearance in the second century has been regarded, as has almost everything in Roman art, in two diametrically opposed ways. Some scholars have seen it as a totally original product of the Italic world; others view it as a simple importation from the Greek world. A glance at the plan of the Hellenistic-Roman dwelling shows, however, that it is just that: the result of the juxtaposition of an Italic house with atrium and a Hellenistic house with peristyle. It is again a phenomenon of assimilation. The first examples merely mix elements from both traditions. Only later is a new type created in which the various elements are seen to merge perfectly. Roman private architecture has a history similar to that of the other arts, from monumental architecture to sculpture and painting.

That one part of the house, surrounding the peristyle, is of Greek origin is shown first of all by the Greek terms which were used to describe it: *oecus* (sitting room), *diaeta* (bedroom), *peristilium* (court or portico with columns), etc. Even the so-called Pompeian painting styles, and the decoration of the house — unlike the structural elements and the building technique — clearly are Greek in origin. The oldest of them, the First Style mentioned above, was a common style of wall decoration in Greece and the Hellenistic cities from the fourth century B.C. onward.

One principal objection made to this formulation of the development of the Roman house is that, in Greece and in the principal Hellenistic cities, there is nothing similar to what is found in Italy. The dwellings there almost never equal those of Pompeii and Herculaneum, either in size or in decorative richness. Yet very little remains of the residential areas of the large Hellenistic cities, from Antioch to Seleucia to Alexandria, and the preservation of the Campanian cities themselves is due to an extraordinary event, the eruption of Vesuvius in A.D. 79. Above all, though, the model for the aristocratic Hellenistic-Roman house is not to be found so much in the common Greek dwelling as in the palaces of the Hellenistic sovereigns. An example is still standing at Pergamon. It is fairly clear that the economic power of a rich landowner, or a banker, or a tax administrator, must have been at least as great as a senator's, and Polybius reports that a Roman senator's patrimony could be compared in Greece only to a king's. This is less surprising if it is recalled that the Roman conquest had drained almost all the wealth of the Mediterranean into Italy.

This can be confirmed by examining some Pompeian houses, particularly the "House of the Faun." Its size alone is indicative of its importance. It occupies an entire block, a lot of about 6500 square yards, slightly less than the size of the so-called "Palace of Columns" at Ptolemais (certainly the Ptolemaic governor's house), and much larger than the king's palace at Pergamon. The building has two atriums and two peristyles, one of which is particularly large — 138 by 128 feet (Ptolemais palace: 95 feet by 82 feet; Pergamon palace: 115 feet by 115 feet). Still more impressive is the high level of decoration. An *exedra*, or semicircular recess, included among the two peristyles, was paved with the celebrated "Mosaic of Alexander" (now housed in the Naples National Museum), one of the most elaborate and finely made examples from the Hellenistic world. It was executed in the second century B.C. by a Greek artist, probably from Alexandria. Smaller mosaics of similar high quality decorated other parts of the house. A small bronze statue of a satyr (rather than a faun) was set at the center of the impluvium and gave the house its name. (The impluvium was the basin in the center of the atrium to catch rainwater from the open roof.) The name of the house's owner is unknown. He

THE FIRST USE OF MARBLE IN PRIVATE HOUSES IN ROME

The first person at Rome who covered the whole of the walls of his house with marble, according to Cornelius Nepos, was Mamurra, who dwelt upon the Caelian Hill, a member of the equestrian order, and a native of Formiae, who had been praefect of the engineers under C. Caesar in Gaul. Such was the individual, that nothing may be wanting to the indignity of the example, who first adopted this practice; the same Mamurra, in fact, who has been so torn to pieces in the verses of Catullus of Verona. Indeed, his own house proclaimed more loudly than Catullus could proclaim it, that he had come into possession of all that Gallia Comata had had to possess. For Nepos adds, as well, that he was the first to have all the columns of his house made of nothing but solid marble, and that, too, marble of Carystus or of Luna.

M. Lepidus, who was consul with Q. Catulus, was the first to have the lintels of his house made of Numidian marble, a thing for which he was greatly censured; he was consul in the year of Rome, 676. This is the earliest instance that I can find of the introduction of Numidian marble; not in the form of pillars, however, or of slabs, as was the case with the marble of Carystus, above-mentioned, but in blocks, and that too, for the comparatively ignoble purpose of making the thresholds of doors. Four years after this Lepidus, L. Lucullus was consul; the same person who gave its name, it is very evident, to the Lucullan marble; for, taking a great fancy to it, he introduced it at Rome. While other kinds of marble are valued for their spots or their colours, this marble is entirely black. It is found in the island of Melos, and is pretty nearly the only marble that has taken its name from the person who first introduced it. Among these personages, Scaurus, in my opinion, was the first to build a theater with walls of marble: but whether they were only coated with slabs of marble or were made of solid blocks highly polished, such as we now see in the Temple of Jupiter Tonans, in the Capitol, I cannot exactly say: for, up to this period, I cannot find any vestiges of the use of marble slabs in Italy.

THE FIRST PAVEMENTS USED IN ROME

The first pavements, in my opinion, were those now known to us as barbaric and subtegulan pavements, a kind of work that was beaten down with the rammer: at least if we may form a judgment from the name that has been given to them. The first diamonded pavement at Rome was laid in the Temple of Jupiter Capitolinus, after the commencement of the Third Punic War. That pavements had come into common use before the Cimbric War, and that a taste for them was very prevalent, is evident from the line of Lucilius —

"With checquered emblems
        like a pavement marked."

Mosaic pavements were first introduced in the time of Sylla; at all events, there is still in existence a pavement, formed of small segments, which he ordered to be laid down in the Temple of Fortune, at Praeneste. Since his time, these mosaics have left the ground for the arched roofs of houses, and they are now made of glass. This, however, is but a recent invention; for there can be no doubt that, when Agrippa ordered the earthenware walls of the hot baths, in the Thermae which he was building at Rome, to be painted in encaustic, and had the other parts coated with pargetting, he would have had the arches decorated with mosaics in glass, if the use of them had been known; or, at all events, if from the walls of the Theater of Scaurus, where it figured, as already stated, glass had by that time come to be used for the arched roofs of apartments.

PLINY THE ELDER: *Natural History* (XXXVI)

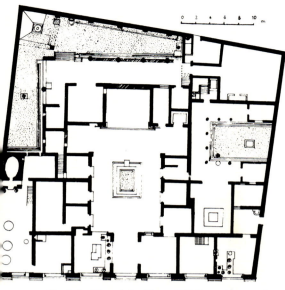

Pompeii: Plan of the House of Sallust. An example of the Italic atrium-type house (third century B.C.).

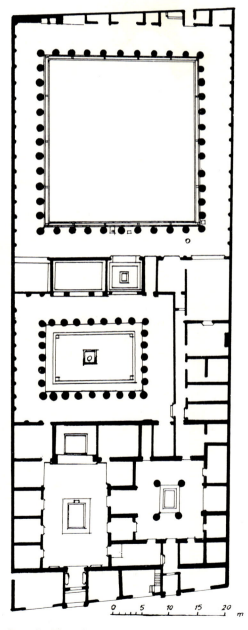

Pompeii: Plan of the House of the Faun (second century B.C.).

was probably one of the local aristocrats, or a landowner who became rich dealing in wine. At any rate the house is a magnificent example of the economic and cultural level of a rich Campanian of the second century B.C. Other houses, less elaborate but equally elegant, may be found at Pompeii and Herculaneum. In Herculaneum the so-called "House of the Samnite" has a magnificent monumental atrium with two sets of columns, an architectural style to be found in the Hellenistic Palace of Columns at Ptolemais.

The Private House in Rome

Some houses of the late second century B.C., with decorations in primitive Second Style, have been discovered in Rome on the Palatine. The best-preserved and most well-known is the so-called "House of the Griffin," built around 100 B.C. and then covered up during the time of Domitian by construction of the *Domus Flavia*. The house is of modest size, especially when compared to the larger Pompeian houses. The Palatine was, however, the most sought-after residential zone in Rome. Land was extremely expensive, as were the houses. A relatively modest house there would certainly be more costly than the houses of a small provincial center such as Pompeii, or the larger suburban villas. Cicero's correspondence gives interesting proof of this. His house on the Palatine, which he bought from Crassus in 62 B.C., cost him 3,500,-000 sesterces, whereas his Villa Tusculanum was worth only about 900,000 sesterces. In fact, even after Clodius had destroyed them, they were valued by the consul at 2,000,000 and 500,000 sesterces respectively. Cicero's Villa Formianum was worth even less; on that same occasion it was valued at 250,000 sesterces. In comparison, the lovely house of Rabirius, in Naples, was sold in 68 B.C. for 130,000 sesterces, according to Cicero.

The beautiful houses in Pompeii must have cost even less. The price of oil in Rome in Cicero's time can serve as a measure of comparison. It cost two or three sesterces a liter. In Pompeii at the beginning of the Imperial Age, a *modius* of wheat (about fifteen pounds) cost three sesterces (and one pound of bread cost about five-eighths of a sesterce); a liter of oil cost about three sesterces; a mule 520 sesterces; two slaves, 5,048 sesterces. (It would not be too far from the truth to calculate the value of the sesterce in this period at about fifty U.S. cents.)

Both the richness and the esthetic level of dwellings at Rome increased rapidly from the end of the second century. They reached their peak about the middle of the first century. What the ancient writers have to say about the use of marble, columns, mosaics, and paintings in the houses of people like Crassus, Clodius, and Scaurus smacks of the fabulous. Yet certain remains verify their accounts. For example, some fragments of a mosaic with a fish, which come from the Vio Panisperna, can be dated at around the beginning of the first century B.C. They represent one of the most refined examples of Hellenistic art, on the same level as the mosaics preserved in Pompeii's House of the Faun (where, incidentally, a square mosaic piece with the same subject has been discovered). Comparison with a similar mosaic in the lower part of the Palestrina sanctuary, probably also executed in this period, permits the attribution of all these fragments to the shop of Alexandrian artisans.

There is evidence of the presence of Alexandrian artists in Rome as early as the first half of the second century B.C. In fact, in 165 B.C., it is known that Demetrius, an Alexandrian painter who had moved to Rome, entertained King Ptolemy VI Philometor, then in exile. This painter is remembered as the "topographer," which, reasoning etymologically, probably means "landscape painter." Painters such as Demetrius are given credit for introducing landscape painting into Rome; it is amply developed in wall paintings of the Second Style.

Above:
Rome: Fragment of a mosaic with fish, from Via Panisperna. Beginning of the first century B.C. As in the case of an identical example at Palestrina, this is a work executed in Rome by Greek artists. It is remarkable for the refinement and variety of its colors and tones. (Antiquario Communale, Rome.)

Right:
Pompeii: House of the Golden Cupids. The peristyle. Built during Nero's time, the house belonged to Gneus Pompeius Abitus. The colonnade, with marble decorations hanging from the architrave, surrounds the garden. The house is one of the most interesting in Pompeii from the Julian-Claudian Age.

Pompeii: Plan of the Forum
1 *Main Square*
2 *Basilica*
3 *Temple of Apollo*
4 *Temple of Jupiter Capitolinus*
5 *Food market (macellum)*
6 *Temple of the Lares*
7 *Temple of Vespasian*
8 *Eumachia Building*
9 *Comitium (municipal elections)*
10 *Hall of the Duumvirs*
11 *Curia*
12 *Hall of the Aediles*

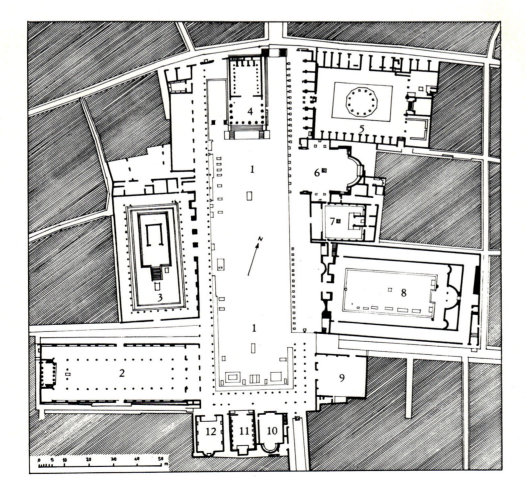

AUGUSTUS DESCRIBES HIS WORKS

I built: the Curia, and the Chalcidicum which adjoins it, the Temple of Apollo on the Palatine and its colonnades, the Temple of Divus Julius, the Lupercal, the Colonnade by the Circus Flaminius (which I allowed to be called the Porticus Octavia, from the name of the Octavius who built an earlier colonnade on the same site), the imperial box in the Circus Maximus, the Temple of Jupiter Feretrius, on the Capitol, and also that of Jupiter Tonans, the Temple of Quirinus, the Temples of Minerva and of Juno Regina and of Jupiter the Giver of Freedom on the Aventine, the Temple of the Lares on the summit of the Sacred Way, the Temple of the Penates on the Velia, the Temple of Juventas, the Temple of Magna Mater on the Palatine.

I repaired the Capitol and the Theater of Pompeius — both works calling for lavish expenditure — without any inscription of my own name. I repaired water conduits which had become derelict with age in very many places: I doubled the Aqua Marcia by enriching its flow from a new source. The Forum Julium, and the Basilica between the Temples of Castor and of Saturn — works which had been begun and carried forward by my Father — I brought to completion. When the Basilica Julia was destroyed by fire I began its restoration on an enlarged site . . . giving instructions that my heirs should complete it if I did not live to do so. As Consul for the sixth time and on the authority of the Senate, I restored eighty-two temples of the gods within the City, neglecting none that then stood in need of repair. In my seventh consulship I repaired the Via Flaminia from Rome to Ariminum, together with all its bridges except Pons Milvius and Pons Minucius.

From the spoils of war, I built the Temple of Mars Ultor and the Forum of Augustus on land which I owned in person. I built the Theater by the Temple of Apollo, on land which was mostly bought from private owners, which should bear the name of my son-in-law, M. Marcellus.

AUGUSTUS: *Res Gestae* (19–21)

Roman state cult, but completely lacking in any true religious content. All of Augustus' actions to restore old and forgotten cults, ancient offices deprived of any function, archaeological objects of every kind, must be seen and understood in this light. The elaborately public display of simplicity, the laws against luxury — perfectly useless, when they did not actually have the opposite effect — and those laws whose purpose was to reestablish public morality, had the same root.

On the other hand, the reestablishment of peace, the centralization of power and of the administration, brought many benefits to the structure of the Empire, especially economic ones. No longer subject to the whims of governors who were above criticism or judgment, the provinces flourished once again, and Italy itself went through a period of revival, although it was short-lived.

The most impressive phenomenon of this era was the intense colonization, especially in Western Europe. Territories such as Gaul, Spain, North Africa, the Rhine and Danube areas, passed with extraordinary speed from a protohistorical structure to a phase of urban civilization. The pre-Italic castles were abandoned and urban centers, joining several villages, grew up. There was at first something artificial in this sharp socioeconomic change. It had been planned in the highest echelons of the government with the evident aim of culturally unifying the Empire. Nonetheless, its success was immense and definitive; the birth of modern Europe is to a large extent connected with it.

The unification of power in the hands of one person had remarkable consequences for Roman culture. Augustus returned to the "moderate" tradition of Scipio Emilianus and his circle, but in a regime of absolute power. Without any serious political or ideological competition to counteract it — excluding the very first years of Augustus' rule — this cultural policy had an extraordinarily wide-ranging effect. Even today Augustus' influence on Roman culture can be seen at every turn, in every field, from literature, to architecture and sculpture, to the most anonymous of the minor arts. The truth is that Augustus succeeded in controlling the culture of the Empire through his centralized power in Rome. The feat was to serve as a model and inspiration in numerous later historical situations.

Augustus lost no time in taking up the pen himself, moreover, and using it as a political and propagandistic weapon, before employing others for the same purpose. Besides those writings that have not been preserved, he wrote the short autobiographical piece called *Res gestae*, or *Monumentum Ancyranum*, since the most complete copy was discovered in Ancyra (modern-day Ankara). It was inscribed on bronze tablets set at the entrance to his tomb, as has been mentioned. In style, the *Res Gestae* strikes the same falsely objective note as Caesar's *Commentaries*. It is an "official report" of the facts. Very few overt value judgments are included, but those few are placed strategically. An almost perfectly unreliable version of events results, yet its penetrative force is demonstrated by the fact that it has ended as the only version, and is used even in school textbooks.

Programs of Augustan Classicism

But the emperor's pen alone, however authoritative, could not establish a tradition. The Ministry of Culture was placed in the hands of Maecenas, a descendant of Etruscan aristocrats, whose vast culture expressed itself not so much in personal works as through his ability to discover talented people who could be hitched to the Augustan wagon. The operation was more successful than could have been hoped. Maecenas' "team" was none other than Virgil, Horace, and Titus Livy, the historian who, with the requisite breadth and the masterly style necessary, dedicated himself to writing the "definitive" Roman history. It would be excessive and unjust to say that Livy or Virgil or Horace acted in bad faith. In fact, the Augustan program of pacification had earned the unconditional support of the generation that lived through the last phase of the civil wars. Nor was there any real political alternative. The partisans of the Republic had a program, but it scarcely served the purpose. It offered only an old-fashioned formula of government whose inadequacy had already been amply demonstrated.

Virgil was a small landowner of the Po region, a member of the Italic middle class, and the *Aeneid* expresses, on a high artistic level, the adherence of that class to the Augustan program of pacification and reorganization. Even though the work was realized in good faith, its propagandistic aspect is nonetheless clear. There is a consistency, even in the details, between some parts of the poem and certain accomplishments of the Augustan Age in architecture and the figurative arts. The catalogue of heroes and of Augustus' predecessors, for example, found in the sixth book of the *Aeneid*, corresponds perfectly to the gallery of portraits set in the porticoes of the Augustan Forum, from Aeneas to Caesar, each with his own "eulogy" written in the traditional style, as in the tomb of the Scipios. It is impossible to believe that the Forum of Augustus and the *Aeneid* were independent productions. It would seem, in fact, that the *Aeneid* came first.

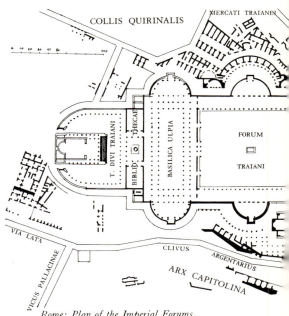
Rome: Plan of the Imperial Forums.

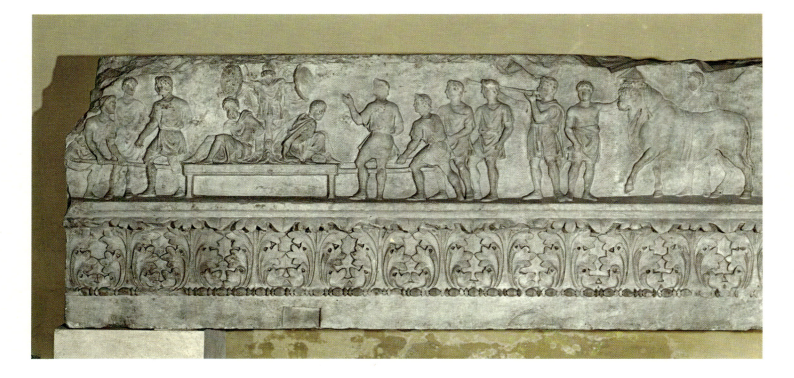

In the figurative arts, as in literature, the style adopted was an imitation of the classical. This was not the first time such a thing had occurred, of course. The first adoption of classicism in Rome — that is, a style drawing on the inspiration of Greek art of the fifth and fourth centuries B.C. — took place during the second century B.C., after the conquest of Greece, as noted earlier. Augustus followed the example of Scipio Emilianus' generation, but with the great consistency and systematization made possible by a more favorable political situation. Here again he set an example. The art of the Augustan Age is the first example of that state classicism whose pomp and splendor surfaced often later in history — in the age of Louis XIV, for instance.

The architectural program was an imposing one. Augustus himself notes, in the *Res Gestae*, that in 29 B.C. alone, eighty-two temples were restored. The destinction between private and public domains was ostentatiously reestablished by the Emperor himself, who in this way linked himself with traditional Roman moralism. According to Sue-

Above:
Rome: Frieze from the cella of the Temple of Apollo Sosianus. Circa 20 B.C. It represents a triumphal scene, perhaps that of Gaius Sosius who had the Temple reerected during the Augustan Age after having triumphed over Judea.

Right:
Rome: Forum of Augustus and Temple of Mars Ultor. Vowed by Augustus in 42 B.C. during the course of the battle of Philippi against Brutus and Cassius, Caesar's assassins, the Temple of Mars Ultor ("the Avenger") was dedicated only in 2 B.C. Like the Temple of Apollo Sosianus, it is made of marble from Carrara.

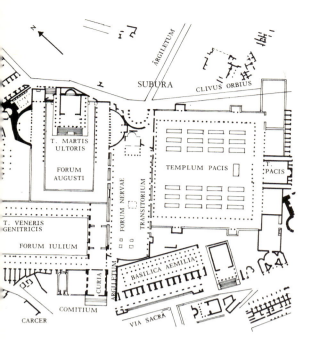

tonius, biographer of the Caesars, Augustus' house on the Palatine, which had belonged to the orator Hortensius, was modest, lacking marble floors and precious furnishings. Since the latest archaeological excavations, it is possible to say that this house is identical with the so-called House of Livia on the Palatine. For Augustus, a new quarter to the south was added, as was the grandiose Temple of Apollo, erected to the memory of the battle of Actium, a kind of private sanctuary for the Emperor. The temple ended as part of the interior of later Imperial palaces.

The public buildings of Augustus' reign were not only great in number, they were grandiose and eloquent. The Emperor boasted that he had found Rome in brick and left it in marble. From a purely architectural point of view, this may have been rather dubious progress. But the quarries of Cararra were worked heavily for the material needed in the Augustan building program, and his was the first era in Roman architecture in which marble was used on a large scale. The Augustan program was even more remarkable for its urban planning, and its reorganization of the structure of the city, than for its individual buildings.

Julius Caesar had formulated gigantic plans. They included a deviation of the Tiber, so that the Vatican area might be joined to the Campus Martius, the huge square where the most important public assemblies and voting ceremonies were held. Most of his projects were interrupted by his sudden death, but what has remained is enough to give an idea of the dictator's clear-sightedness. He had aimed at making old Rome into a capital worthy of comparison with the great eastern cities, Alexandria in particular. Caesar's building and planning had two distinct aspects. The first was innovative, almost revolutionary. The other was directed toward the restoration of all the old buildings connected with the Republican constitution (Augustus, much more prudent, gave precedence to the latter aspect).

One of the innovative plans was Caesar's Forum, begun in 54 B.C., according to one of Cicero's letters. This was a private work, rather than a public work, and was built at the expense of Caesar, who was then consul; the cost of the land alone was an astronomical 100 million sesterces. The Forum was begun in reaction to the initiative of Pompey, who as consul in 55 B.C. had inaugurated in the Campus Martius the first brick theater in Rome and the enormous portico with gardens that bore his name for posterity. Caesar's desire to crush his rival here as well is seen in his initiation of another theater in the same parade ground. (This was finished by Augustus, who dedicated it to the memory of his nephew Marcellus.) The function of Caesar's Forum is clear. It extended and enlarged the old Republican Forum, by then insufficient in size, in the direction of the Campus Martius, and at the same time linked his name with a monumental complex of an entirely new kind, probably taken from Near Eastern models; the historian Appian placed it in relation to the Parthian squares.

During the course of construction, probably after 48 B.C., the Temple of Venus Genetrix was added to the Forum, closing off the end of the square with perfect axial perspective. The apse at the end of the Temple's cella, where the sacred image of the goddess was placed, thus constituted the end and the focus of an obligatory itinerary: the colonnades guided the visitor or worshiper toward the Temple, inside which two other colonnades concentrated his attention on the apse. This was no accident; the cult of the Venus Mother served a dynastic function for Caesar. From the funeral eulogy for his aunt, he remembered the divine origin of the Julia family, which was descended from Aeneas, and hence from Venus, Aeneas' divine mother. The function of this private cult in Caesar's plans is undoubted. He wished to establish a monarchy of the eastern type in Rome, and his sojourn in Egypt had clarified for him the essence of regality. Deification of the sovereign quite clearly played a large part in it, and Caesar's Forum is the monumental reflection of these concepts.

The other aspect of Julius Caesar's construction activity was only apparently opposed to the first. In reality it was complementary. At the same time the Forum was being built, reconstruction of an ancient part of the Campus Martius in monumental form was begun. This sort of project, giving a monumental appearance to a structure whose function was no longer valid, was to become the forte of Augustus. The Augustan program was much less audacious as regards deification than Caesar's, however. Augustus always refused to accept deification during his lifetime, at least in Rome and the West. (He was adored in Egypt, though, as the god Thoth, corresponding to the Greek Hermes and the Roman Mercury, and in the East temples dedicated to Rome and Augustus sprang up everywhere).

The schemes of urban planning begun by Caesar were continued and developed by Augustus. Rome probably had 500,000 inhabitants at this time. Augustus divided the city into fourteen districts, each furnished with particular administrative and technical services; there was one fire-brigade for each two districts, for example. The bed of the Tiber was "mended," set in order and limited in size. The entrances to the ancient city walls attributed to Servius Tullius were reconstruct-

Rome: The Basilica Julia, in the Roman Forum. Begun by Julius Caesar, the building was totally remade by Augustus after a fire, and dedicated to his grandsons Gaius and Lucius Caesar. After the various sacks and destructions it endured up to the Renaissance; only the delineation of the plan remains.

ed; they had served only as topographical landmarks before this time. Agrippa, the friend and close associate of Augustus, brought a new aqueduct to Rome and created the first monumental public baths there, in the Campus Martius, next to the Pantheon, which was built at this time, also by Agrippa. Members of the most important Roman families were invited to collaborate in the program, and for the last time names other than the Emperor's were connected with public buildings. Cornificus reconstructed the Temple of Diana on the Aventine; Balbus, the theater named after him in the Campus Martius; Asinius Pollio, the ancient "Atrium of Liberty," where slaves were freed, as well as the first public library in Rome.

The activity of the Emperor Augustus was on a much larger scale. Among the most important structures he raised were the Portico of Octavia, erected in place of the older Portico of Metellus and furnished with two libraries, one for Greek and one for Latin; the Portico of Livia on the Esquiline; the Theater of Marcellus; the Temple of Apollo on the Palatine; and an enormous number of other sanctuaries, either built anew or reconstructed. The widening of the public zone of the forums was continued by the creation of the Forum of Augustus, this also built at the private expense of the Emperor. At its end, in a position analogous to that of the Temple of Venus Genetrix in Caesar's Forum, the Temple of Mars Ultor ("the avenger" — of Caesar's assassination) was built. The dynastic intention of the temple in Caesar's Forum persisted in the newer monument, although it assumed there a more traditional form, less distasteful to the Roman mentality. The statues of progenitors of the Julia family, from Aeneas on — the kings of Alba and Rome, the greatest personages of the

Rome: The *Ara Pacis* of Augustus. 13-9 B.C. Frieze from the south side. From left to right: priests (the figures with unusual headgear); Agrippa with his head veiled, followed by his wife Julia (the daughter of Augustus). Between them is one of their sons, probably Lucius Caesar. Then come Tiberius, Antonia and her husband Drusus with their son Germanicus, and the Enobarbus family.

But what is it that I am first to prohibit,
what excess retrench to the ancient standard?
Am I to begin with that of our country seats,
spacious without bounds; and with the number
of domestics, from various countries? or with
the quantity of silver and gold? or with the
pictures, and statues of brass, the wonders of
art? or with vestments, promiscuously worn
by men and women? or with what is peculiar
to the women — those precious stones, —
for the purchase of which our coin is carried
into foreign or hostile nations?... Why then
did parsimony prevail of old? It was because
every one was a law to himself — it was because
we were then the citizens of one city; nor afterward, while our dominion was confined to
Italy, had we the same incentives to voluptuous-
ness. By foreign conquests we learned to waste
the property of others, and by civil wars to con-
sume our own. How small is the evil of which
the aediles warn us! how lightly does it weigh
in the balance with others! It is wonderful
that nobody lays before the senate that Italy
stands in need of foreign supplies; that the
lives of the Roman people are daily exposed
to the mercy of uncertain seas and tempests;
were it not for our supplies from the provinces
—supplies by which the masters, and their
slaves, and their estates, are maintained —
will our groves, forsooth, and villas maintain
us? This duty, conscript fathers, devolves
upon the prince; and if it were neglected,
the utter ruin of the state would follow.

TACITUS: *The Annals* (III:537-41)

Roman Republic — were placed in niches along the Forum's two
lateral porticoes. At the end of the series, in a grandiose hall, a gigantic
statue of Augustus was erected, probably after his death, clearly demon-
strating how all the events of Roman history providentially tended
to concentrate on one point: the person of the Emperor. It was he
who gathered up, epitomized and yet conciliated all the contrasts
and struggles of Rome in a supreme pacification, above all ranks and
parties. The ideological program was no less clear or persuasive for
having been expressed in marble and bronze rather than in writing.

Ara Pacis Augustae

For an understanding of the cultural and ideological climate in
Augustan Rome, the *Ara Pacis Augustae*, the Altar of Augustan Peace,
is equally interesting. The votive offering for it was made in 13 B.C.
and the monument itself was inaugurated in 9 B.C. It was situated
in the Campus Martius, the principal center of Augustan building
activity. Excavated in various stages and finally recomposed in 1938,
the altar is the most important example of official Roman sculpture
of the period. The structural conception is interesting; the marble
altar is placed at the center of a quadrangular enclosure, also of
marble, which has two openings. The enclosure is evidently an imitation of a wooden structure; on the interior the lower part is an imitation
of a wooden floor, and the sculptured hanging garlands of the upper
part are probably copies of the real garlands that adorned the tem-
porary enclosure erected for the votive offering.

Rome: The Mausoleum of Augustus. Erected in the Campus Martius after the battle of Actium, the monument, over 285 feet in diameter, housed the tombs of the entire Julian-Claudian family. It was conceived, as the name suggests, as an imitation of the great dynastic sepulchers of the Hellenistic sovereigns. At the sides of the entranceway stood two obelisks (now in the Piazza del Quirinale and the Piazza dell' Esquiliano) and the bronze tablets containing the text of Augustus' autobiography.

The outside of the enclosure presents a different, and much less consistent, aspect. Rich decorations of spiral form, with an acanthus motif, and populated with animals, fill the lower part of all four sides. In the upper portion of the two long sides, unbroken by entrances, a procession is depicted, most likely that in which all the imperial family participated during the sacrifice connected with the consecration of the altar. On the shorter sides, with the two entrances, there are four sculptured marble panels. Two of these depict mythical events connected with the legend of the foundation of Rome: Aeneas sacrificing to the Penates in Lavinium; and the *Lupercalia*, the scene in the sacred grotto at the foot of the Palatine, with Romulus and Remus being suckled by the wolf. On the other side there are two symbolic scenes. In one, the goddess Roma is seated on a pile of weapons, representing the final victory of the city and the imperial dominion based on military force; in the other, the Earth, represented as a woman of ample proportions, with two children in her lap, and flanked by symbolic figures of water and air, is placed in the midst of luxuriant growth and vegetation. The symbolism is transparent in this case as well: these are the material benefits and the prosperity that derive from the reestablishment of peace.

The lack of an organic principal or a sense of organization in the monument is evident even from this brief description. Realistic, mythological, and symbolic representations, as well as purely ornamental material, are placed together without any connection except their propagandistic function. As often happens in figurative art of this period, the weight of the ceremonial intentions overwhelms any possibility of coherent artistic realization. The defect is much less evident in literature, perhaps because of the greater social dignity, hence the greater liberty, that writers enjoyed. Compared to writers, sculptors and painters, since they worked with their hands, were considered little more than laborers. The split between intellectual and manual work, theory and practice, was inevitably great in a slave society such as that of the Augustan Age.

From a formal point of view the *Ara Pacis*, like all official art in the Augustan period, is an example of classically-minded academicism, correct, technically irreproachable, but without a speck of vitality. To reach this state, the various aspects of Greek art that had mixed

Rome: The Tomb of Cecilia Metella, on the Appian Way. About 20 B.C. About the time of the Mausoleum of Augustus, the use of monumental tombs, often surmounted by a tumulus, became widespread. One of the best examples is the Tomb of Cecilia Metella, daughter of a Metellus and wife of a Crassus. In the Middle Ages the tomb was transformed into a tower in the castle built along the Appian Way by the Caetani. The merlons visible in the upper part of the edifice date back to this period.

Following pages:

Rome: The House of Livia on the Palatine. The *Tablinum*. Recent excavations have demonstrated that this building is part of a complex that most likely was the residence of Augustus. The paintings decorating the walls of the Tablinum are among the finest examples of Second Style wall painting, and may be dated at the beginning of the Augustan Age.

with Roman art — "illusionism" and Hellenistic naturalism, the neoclassic that harked back to Attic models — and even Roman plebeian art, were all absorbed, manipulated, restored, and painstakingly, carefully devitalized. To unify so many disparate, contrasting elements stylistically was obviously impossible. They were instead eclectically placed one beside the other, in a fashion coldly correct, but little more.

Nevertheless, this art had the merit, recognizable also in the poetry of Horace, to which it is spiritually akin, of establishing a formal grammar; every self-respecting neo-classicism aspires to do the same. The result was an "average," "bourgeois" style, without strain or contortion if also without enthusiasm or impetus. It constituted for centuries an obligatory reference point, not only for the culture of the Roman Empire but for European culture in general.

Proof of this is the fact that, at least in urban areas, Augustan art penetrated deeply, reaching into every aspect of building. Thus, the characteristically archaic style of the Mausoleum of Augustus — built in the form of a tumulus, like the tombs of Etruscan noblemen — became the model for numerous private sepulchers, such as the famous tomb of Cecilia Metella on the Appian Way. The style of the *Ara Pacis* was an official style; it served as the model for the production of decorative sculpture on an infinite number of funerary altars, columns, and chapels that have been preserved.

Minor Arts in the Augustan Period

Finally, even in the so-called minor arts the Augustan period has left its indelible mark. Silver vases, cameos, jewels, and even the most common ceramics show their direct dependence on official art. The red ceramics of Arezzo, first produced in the last years of Julius Caesar's life, became the model for ceramics through the entire Imperial period, but it was under Augustus that their production reached almost industrial proportions. The figures on the ceramics were cast in a mold. They show great technical skill and formal correctness, as well as the academic coldness typical of the art of this period. The really extraordinary diffusion of these Arezzo ceramics (specimens have been found as far from Rome as southern India) illustrate the spread of Greco-Roman artistic culture to countries that up to then had been completely untouched by it.

As in the Republican period, the private world must be considered separately. Yet the story is about the same. The development of wall painting can be followed through the rich documentation of Herculaneum and Pompeii, and through some work in Rome itself. During the first century B.C. the type of wall decoration called Second Style became widespread. Characterized by a naturalism with the tendency to "break through" the wall, either with architectural perspective or scenes of landscape, it was really purely Hellenistic rather than Roman, and in fact represents one of the most notable contributions of Hellenism to Roman art. It continued to be used in the first years of the Augustan Age; the House of Livia on the Palatine is a perfect example of the mature Second Style.

In the Villa Farnesiana, discovered at the end of the nineteenth century near the right bank of the Tiber, the paintings (now in the Roman National Museum) are more eclectic in character. Besides parts that are still fully naturalistic, and others belonging to the more typical late Hellenistic "impressionism," there are also linear and schematic renderings, and even paintings of an archaic flavor that hark back to Greek art of the fifth century B.C. The different elements are not distinct, but they are linked to one another indifferently. This is the intellectual phenomenon typical of bourgeois art such as that of the *Ara Pacis*, although in a different environment. The decorative work of the Villa Farnesiana can be dated at least twenty or forty years after the paintings in the House of Livia, probably about 20 B.C.

The Third Style originated around 15 B.C. Characterized by extreme simplification of architectural elements, which assume a graceful, threadlike aspect, by growing use of monochrome surfaces, and by a technique that could be defined as miniaturist, this again was a classical style, and ran parallel to that in vogue in sculpture and architecture at the same time. The use of large paintings with mythological subjects continued, although there was less taste in such work for third dimension and perspective. Representations of gardens, free from any architectural frame, were popular as well; the best example found was at the Villa of Livia at Prima Porta, on the Via Flaminia (and is now in the Roman National Museum).

Art of the Tiberian Age

During the course of his long reign, Augustus was able to complete a profound reorganization of the state. So thorough was his work, so clearly was the way marked out for his successors, that they found it difficult, if not impossible, to change it. This was true not only of official culture but of politics. The two were closely connected. In politics Caligula and Nero sets out to reform the Augustan edifice by attempting to change the Roman state to something resembling an eastern monarchy, but they failed miserably. The public art of the entire Julian-Clau-

Prima Porta: The Villa of Livia. Wall painting of a garden (now on display at the Roman National Museum). Last part of the first century B.C.

dian dynasty, except for the reign of Nero, its last representative, differed hardly at all from that of the Augustan period, except in its nuances. It must be noted, however, that documentation of the Julian-Claudian Era is very scarce, especially in the urban context.

In private art, however, great differences occur from period to period in the dynasty. This can be said not primarily because the documentation is greater, as might be supposed, but rather because the personalities of the various emperors had scope for expression in areas where state policy did not intervene, at least in a direct way.

Developments of this kind began immediately with Augustus' successor Tiberius (A.D. 14–37). Although completely different in character from Augustus, Tiberius found himself compelled to continue his predecessor's policies. The result was the tortuosity, the near-maniacal displays of irritability, which characterized Tiberius as a ruler. His taste and culture led him to prefer "high" Hellenistic art over neo-Attic-classicism. This fact is pointed out by ancient writers, and can be clearly seen in the monuments connected with his name. In the temple reconstructions he carried out before he became emperor — the Temple of Castor and Pollux in the Forum and the Temple of Concord at the foot of the Capitol — there is already a difference in style from the edifices built under Augustus' direction, such as the Temple of Mars Ultor. Tiberius' propensity was for "baroque" Hellenistic models from Asia Minor, a taste confirmed by the choice of sculpture for the Temple of Concord. All the works were by artists belonging to the early or middle Hellenistic periods. But the phenomenon is evident above all in the Emperor's private villas, in Capri, where he transferred his court, never again to return to Rome, and in Sperlonga (only recently discovered). The choice of sites is significant in itself. His propensity was for sea settings, for isolation in literary idleness. Tiberius seems to have despised Rome. For some years before becoming emperor, he lived in Rhodes, and his choice of retreats closely resembled that of personages in the late Republican period, such as Lucullus and Hortensius. Tiberius had an affinity for their culture, and indeed went to die in Lucullus' villa at Miseno, as noted earlier. The fact takes on an almost symbolic value.

The architecture and decoration of the Capri and Sperlonga villas are characterized by a marked taste for landscape that is a mixture of the natural and the artificial. Grottoes were transformed into nympheums, even the famous Blue Grotto, and decorated with statues. At Sperlonga these were original Greek statues, Rhodian, of the late Hellenistic Age. The choice of pieces is interesting, too. The sculptures depict scenes from the *Odyssey*, related to the nearby localities of Gaeta and Circeo, where two of Ulysses' most famous adventures took place. (The mixture of the artificial and the natural is very much akin to the taste displayed in the Renaissance art of sixteenth century gardens and villas.)

A new feature in the decoration of Tiberius' villas was the wall mosaic, which was destined for a great future. Introduced at the end of the Republican Age, this technique became remarkably widespread from the Tiberian Age on to the end of the first century A.D., particularly for decoration of the walls of nympheums and fountains. Mosaics have been found in Capri and Sperlonga, in Nero's *Domus Aurea*, in numerous houses at Pompeii and Herculaneum, especially in the last phase, between the earthquake of A.D. 63 and the eruption of A.D. 79. In one case the wall mosaic is to be found in a tomb, belonging to Pomponius Hylas, near the Via Latina, which probably dates from the Tiberian Age. A monumental specimen, with a representation of a ship in port, decorated the great nympheum of a patrician house on the Quirinal, which may have belonged to Avidius Quietus, a personage of the age of Domitian. In the prevailing use of this technique for the decoration of apses, which occurred often in nympheums, and of large surfaces, the precursors of Byzantine and medieval wall mosaics can be seen.

Above:
Rome: *Colombarium* of Pomponius Hylas. A small replica of a dovecote in a tomb of the Tiberian Age in the Aurelian Wall near Via Latina. It is noted for its frescoes and mosaics, on which is recorded the name of the owner.

Opposite page:
Rome: The *Domus Aurea* of Nero. Above, detail from the decorative painting on a ceiling. Below, a room in the eastern section with rich Fourth Style pictorial decoration.

The Works of Nero

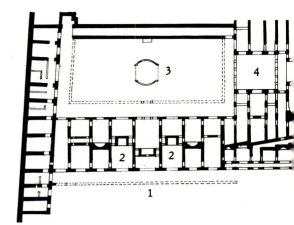

It is worth mentioning, with regard to the residences and property of the emperors, that between the reigns of Augustus and Nero the noble Republican families were slowly eliminated. The process had important economic consequences, and went forward most prominently during the first decades of the Imperial Age, but it had been started already by the triumvirate of Octavius, Mark Antony, and Lepidus, with the proscriptions of 43 B.C., in which Cicero was one of the men killed. The political objective was to eliminate, even physically, the class that had held power. But the economic aim of the policy was no less important. In the first years of the Imperial Age, most of the great villas that had grown up on the hills east of Rome, from the Pincio to the Esquiline, passed into the Imperial domain, including those of Sallust, Pompey, and Maecenas. Outside Rome the same thing happened; the most pleasant parts of the coast and the most beautiful islands became Imperial property: Baia, Capri, the coast between Gaeta and Terracina. Along the coast, where the Sperlonga villa was built, there is an inscription that mentions an attorney whose job it was to administer the Imperial domain of Formia, Gaeta, and Fondi. This system of state ownership, which had both good and bad points, was extended in the middle and late Imperial Age to include most of the sources of production. The brick factories are one example; they will be considered later.

It was the possession of such vast areas of urban land that allowed the megalomaniacal emperor, Nero, to plan and construct two gigantic royal palaces, the *Domus Transitoria* and the *Domus Aurea*. Very little remains of the *Domus Transitoria*, which extended way beyond the confines of the Palatine, the traditional residence of the emperors. There are some frescoes with Homeric scenes, which represent one of the most ancient known examples of "Fourth Style" painting. When the *Domus Transitoria* was destroyed by the fire of A.D. 64, Nero began to build a larger palace extending from the Palatine to the Esquiline and Coelian hills, taking up most of the central area of the city. Indignant Romans immediately circulated epigrams, and pasquinades lampooned this move. One, mentioned by Suetonius, invites the Quirites to emigrate to Veii, since "Rome is already occupied by one house."

The *Domus Aurea* was not so much a palace as a grandiose villa, with pavilions set in planted areas. These had ponds, paths, forests, and cultivated fields, all laid out according to the rules of the most evolved garden art. A similar example of such a complex is Hadrian's Villa at Tivoli, which also served as the site of the Imperial court, but which had the added advantage, evidently of no importance to Nero, of being outside the urban center. The only part of this elaborate residence which remains lies on the Oppian Hill, protected by the Baths of Trajan which were built over it. The plan shows two sections quite different from each other, both in structure and architectural character. The section to the west is simpler than the section to the east, which has a great deal of movement and animation. Perhaps the separate hands of the two architects, Severus and Celer, can be recognized in the two sections. According to Pliny the Elder, they were the designers of the complex.

The name of the painter who did the major part of the decoration is also known; he was Fabullus or Famulus (Pliny's writings give both spellings), the only personality in Roman painting of this time who is known by name. The decoration of the *Domus Aurea*, which at best is poorly preserved, is one of the most interesting examples of Fourth Style painting, otherwise known so well through work at Pompeii and Herculaneum. The Fourth Style is actually a complicated and baroque version of the fantastic architectural motifs already seen in the Second Style. Ornamental exuberance is common to both. Fourth Style breaks out above all in work of the Flavian period, following

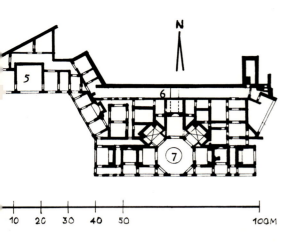

Pages 104-105:
Rome: The Colosseum, seen from the slopes of the Palatine (in the foreground, the Arch of Constantine). The outer measurements of this edifice, oval in shape, are 620 feet by 513 feet. Its height is 158 feet. The collapse of a part of the external ring allows a view of the travertine supporting structure, built prior to the rest of the building, which was completed with brick.

Pages 106-107:
Rome: The Colosseum, interior view. The complex system of underground chambers, used for the most important functions and services of the amphitheater, is visible, since the original floor of the arena has disappeared.

Nero; the break with Augustan classicism could not be sharper. The revaluation of baroque Hellenism, appreciated in the private sphere from Tiberius on, is here brought even into public art, with results that — especially in official sculpture and architecture — were among the most remarkable ever realized by the Romans.

Rome in the Flavian Era; The Colosseum and Domitian's Palace

The civil war that followed Nero's death brought to power the representative of an obscure Sabine family, Flavius Vespasian. Brief though it was, the episode was important in Roman history. Augustus had had to gain the support of the Italic middle classes in his war against Antony, and Vespasian appealed to the provinces against Italy, which had declared itself in favor of his rival, Vitellus. The policy of the Flavians tended to favor the upper strata of the municipal bourgeoisie in the more "Latinized" western provinces. The ancient families of the Republican nobility not only disappeared definitively from the Senate (a process initiated under the Julian-Claudian rulers, as noted earlier), but the families of the newer nobility, that created by Augustus, were also "eliminated."

Developments in the economic situation paralleled the political developments. By this time the decadence of Italy was total. Agricultural production was decreasing; olive oil, for example, which had been one of the chief Italian exports during the late Republican period, was now imported in great quantities from Spain. In the industrial field the production of Aretine pottery stopped and was replaced by products from the ceramic factories of Gaul, which were imported by Italy on a large scale. This development became more and more acute during the course of the second century A.D. When the Roman-Italic state became the "world state," Rome, devoid of any economic "hinterland," became only the parasitical capital of an immense territory in which the provinces took on almost the aspect of separate and autonomous nations. They were the true economic centers of the Empire.

From the artistic point of view as well, the passage from the Julian-Claudian rulers to the Flavians corresponded to a sharp break. In the urban center, large-scale public construction continued; in fact it increased. In this phase some of the most remarkable monuments were built: the Colosseum, the Baths of Titus, Domitian's Stadium, the Forum of Peace, and Nerva's Forum (really built by Domitian). The municipal plebeian art characteristic of central Italy from the end of the Republican to the Julian-Claudian period practically disappeared, however. The end of the production of sculpture to decorate the sepulchers of the Italic bourgeoisie is perhaps the best demonstration of the progressive decline of the class.

On the other hand, the Flavian period, and even more, the second century, mark the rapid development of provincial artistic cultures, with the creation of autonomous "national" artistic traditions. It is possible to speak of a Gallic culture, an African culture, etc. This is particularly noteworthy in the western provinces. Through Rome, they absorbed Hellenistic artistic civilization and developed it in an autonomous, original way, mixing it with local traditions. This phennomenon was the root of the various "Romance" cultures that then formed in the Middle Ages. The course of urban artistic culture in Rome proceeded almost completely independent from this varied and complex evolution in the provinces. It was, however, no longer the reflection of the activities and choices of an articulated society, but rather a culture of the court, more and more determined by the personality of the emperor. There were obviously reciprocal influences between the artistic production in the provinces and that in the urban

center, but it would be a great mistake to consider the art in the provinces a mere reflection of urban art at the periphery of the Empire.

With the Flavians, and even more with Trajan, urban art took on a consistent and homogeneous aspect. The fluctuations in taste that had characterized the Julian-Claudian age diminished. Architecture, freed from the classical forms of Augustan tradition, took up the Republican "thread" in a new way and followed it to the point of realizing quite noteworthy achievements. The most famous urban monument of the period, the Colosseum, also serves as one of the most significant examples of the building techniques used in Rome during the Imperial Age. The work was carried out very quickly: begun in A.D. 77, the building was finished and inaugurated by Titus in 80. Scarcely four years were needed for the realization of one of the most imposing achievements in ancient architecture.

Incredible as it may seem, precise and exhaustive studies of the Colosseum do not exist, but some points have been sufficiently studied and clarified. It is known that the edifice was built in a valley once occupied by a lake belonging to the park of Nero's *Domus Aurea*. This fact has sometimes been cited as an example of the virtuosity of the Flavian architects, but it is probable that in reality it must be regarded as a simple technical expedient to save work. The digging for the amphitheater's foundations would have meant the removal of some 150,000 cubic yards of material. Using the cavity of the lake allowed the architects to eliminate a large part of this work. The Colosseum's greatest novelty lay in its structural conception. First, all the travertine pillars with their related vaults were built — that is, the skeleton support of the edifice, on which the tiers rested. This made it possible for many workers to work at the same time, even during bad weather, as they were literally "indoors." The secondary parts of the construction were quickly finished. The technique is close to that used for modern structures of metal or reinforced concrete.

The activity of the Flavians in the field of public building was not limited to the Colosseum. The Forum of Peace, which Pliny called the most beautiful monument in Rome, was built at the order of Vespasian. Titus, during the course of his brief reign, finished the work on the baths that took his name. They completed the group of buildings in the area around the Colosseum, occupying a part of the *Domus Aurea*. The most active emperor in this period, though, was Domitian, who reigned the longest of all the Flavians, from A.D. 82 to 96. Consistent with his tendency toward a highly centralized, eastern-style state, Domitian was the first emperor after Nero to sponsor a large-scale program of private Imperial building. His father, Vespasian, and his brother Titus, partially in order to make people forget some all-too-recent events, had contented themselves with the already existing edifices and had actively initiated not only the elimination of the remains of the *Domus Aurea* but its replacement by public works. Trajan was to complete the process, which had an obvious political character.

Nevertheless, Domitian built a grandiose palace on the Palatine and numerous villas. The most important, near Lake Albano, is also the most magnificent Imperial villa before Hadrian's time. The name of the emperor's favorite architect is known: he was Rabirius, the builder of the Palatine palace. The *Domus Aurea* had followed more or less the plan of a villa, with isolated pavilions in the center of a garden complex. But the palace of Domitian was a compact block, built in two sections: one, the so-called *Domus Flavia*, on the northwest, was used for receptions and other state functions; the other, the so-called *Domus Augustana*, was used as a residence.

For the construction of the *Domus Augustana* the incline of the Palatine hill was transformed into a stairway. The front of the house, facing the Circus Maximus, consisted of a large *exedra*, behind which there was a peristyle decorated with a fountain. At the end of this peristyle, a group of rooms and two staircases led to the top terrace of the hill

Rome: The *Domus Augustana* on the Palatine. Domitian Age. View of the great lower courtyard, which served as the monumental entranceway to the building, from the side facing the Circus Maximus. At the center is a large fountain with a complicated design. In the background are the upper floors, which elegantly utilize the natural slope of the hill.

THE RECONSTRUCTION OF ROME AFTER THE FIRE OF NERO

Nero appropriated to his own purposes the ruins of his country, and founded upon them a palace; in which the old-fashioned, and, in those luxurious times, common ornaments of gold and precious stones, were not so much the objects of attraction as lands and lakes; in one part, woods like vast deserts; in another part, open spaces and expansive prospects. The projectors and superintendents of this plan were Severus and Celer. . . . But the rest of the old site not occupied by his palace, was laid out, not as after the Gallic fire, without discrimination and regularity, but with the lines of streets measured out, broad spaces left for transit, the height of the buildings limited, open areas left, and porticoes added to protect the front of the clustered dwellings: these porticoes Nero engaged to rear at his own expense, and then to deliver to each proprietor the areas about them cleared. He moreover proposed rewards proportioned to every man's rank and private substance, and fixed a day within which, if their houses, single and clustered, were finished, they should receive them: he appointed the marshes of Ostia for a receptacle of the rubbish, and that the vessels which had conveyed grain up the Tiber should return laden with rubbish; that the buildings themselves should be raised a certain portion of their height without beams, and arched with stone from the quarries of Gabii or Alba, that stone being proof against fire: that over the water springs, which had been improperly intercepted by private individuals, overseers should be placed, to provide for their flowing in greater abundance, and in a greater number of places, for the supply of the public: that every housekeeper should have in his yard means for extinguishing fire; neither should there be party-walls, but every house should be inclosed by its own walls. These regulations, which were favorably received, in consideration of their utility, were also a source of beauty to the new city: yet some there were who believed that the ancient form was more conducive to health, as from the narrowness of the streets and the height of the buildings the rays of the sun were more excluded; whereas now, the spacious breadth of the streets, without any shade to protect it, was more intensely heated in warm weather.

TACITUS: *The Annals* (XV:42-3)

Rome: The *Domus Augustana* on the
Palatine. View of the stadium, which
closed the southern side of the complex.

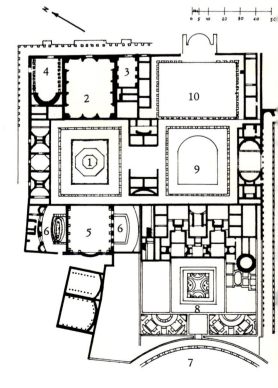

on which another group of rooms surrounded a second peristyle.
The whole was completed, on the southeast side, by a hippodrome —
literally a horse track, but often to be found in villas as a circular
walk.

The *Domus Flavia* consisted of a smaller number of rooms, also set
around a peristyle. There were basically two groups: to the northeast
the *Aula Regia*, flanked by the Basilica and the so-called Lararium;
to the southwest, the grandiose triclinium, or banquet room, flanked
by two nympheums. The chambers in the first group were most certainly the reception complex of the Imperial palace, which was used
for a long time, not only by Domitian but by succeeding emperors.
Because of its central position, as compared to the other Imperial
edifices, its rational arrangement, the variety and boldness of its
architectural solutions (the vault that covered the *Aula Regia* was
probably one of the most grandiose ever realized by Roman architecture), the Domitian complex is the best known example of the Imperial
palace. Again the planning of the building was no accident. Domitian
was a "centralizer," extremely determined and consistent in his

Rome: Plan of the palace of Domitian on the Palatine.
On the left (the Domus Flavia):
1 *Peristyle*
2 *Aula Regia*
3 *Lararium*
4 *Basilica*
5 *Triclinium*
6 *Nympheums*
On the right (the Domus Augustana):
7 *Facade*
8 *Atrium with monumental fountain*
9 *Peristyle*
10 *Peristyle*

affirmation of Imperial power as absolute and divine. He was given the title of *Dominus*, "lord," while still alive.

Domitian was remarkably active in the field of public building as well. His greatest achievement in that field was certainly the reconstruction of the Campus Martius and the Capitol, both ravaged by a terrible fire during the reign of Titus, in A.D. 80. Of those works of which traces remain, the most noteworthy is the stadium, whose site forms the present-day Piazza Navona.

The Emperor wanted his name linked with a Forum as well, the *Forum Transitorium*, but it was inaugurated in A.D. 97, after his death, and took on the name of the emperor Nerva. The remains of this forum display — especially in their architectural decoration — that taste for the baroque so characteristic of late Flavian art. It is to be found also in sculpture, in the admirable reliefs on the Arch of Titus, for example, which depict the triumph of the emperor after the Jewish wars. They were executed after Titus's death, certainly during Domitian's reign.

THE ROMAN UNIVERSE   111

The Works of Trajan

The pinnacle of official Roman sculpture was reached during the reign of the last emperor who had any ambitions of conquest, Trajan, the "new Caesar," under whom the Empire reached its maximum size, after the annexation of Dacia, Arabia, and Mesopotamia. This Emperor's feats were commemorated in an impressive series of monuments, the most remarkable of which was the Forum of Trajan. This was the work of Apollodorus of Damascus who, as a military engineer, had planned the grandiose stone bridge erected over the Danube during the second Dacian war. The fact that the Forum of Trajan took up and brought to a definite solution the problem set by Caesar, of linking the Republican Forum to the Campus Martius, is not without significance. To realize the plan, the saddle of land that linked the Quirinal to the Capitol was razed to the ground, as the inscription on Trajan's Column records. Equally significant from an ideological point of view was the fact that the Emperor undertook, at the same time, the reconstruction of Caesar's Forum. The two projects were inaugurated together. Trajan's Forum was basically a glorification of the Emperor's achievements, the Dacian war in particular. A series of gigantic statues of Dacian prisoners probably decorated the attic of the side porticoes, and a complex of sculptures referring to the same campaign and to its triumph must have embellished the great barrel-vaulted arch that served as the Forum's entrance. The sculptures in the reliefs later used in the Arch of Constantine do not seem to be these, however. A bronze statue of the Emperor mounted on a horse occupied the center of the square, connecting the project even more explicitly to the person of Trajan. Augustus had realized nothing of this scope in his Forum, but the center of Caesar's Forum was also dominated by a statue of the dictator on a horse.

The most noteworthy element of the project, still preserved in its integrity, is the Column of Trajan. It is the earliest example of a monument of which only a few other examples are known — at Rome the Column of Marcus Aurelius; at Constantinople, those of Theodosius and Arcadius. The Column of Trajan was placed in a courtyard between the Basilica Ulpia and the two libraries of the Forum. Its reliefs were certainly more legible then, from the terraces of these adjacent buildings, than they are today, the more so because they were originally painted in rich polychrome. The Column was set in a narrow space; its effect was probably more didactic than monumental, a storied "scroll" that, like the texts in the nearby libraries, served to illustrate in detail the course of the two Dacian wars fought by the Emperor. The documentary wealth of the Column is such that today, given the paucity of texts connected with Trajan's reign, it is the most complete historical record of these wars that now exists. The ideological importance of the monument was also great. The Emperor's ashes were put in a golden urn placed in the base of the monument, a procedure that had probably been planned from the beginning.

With Trajan, historical reliefs reached their maturity. The fact that their documentation regarding his reign is so rich is not fortuitous. From its earliest examples, the historical relief had been connected with the Roman imperialist class. Its function was nothing more or less than the exaltation of conquest. The Emperor-soldier, who stretched the boundaries of the Roman Empire to their maximum extent, could only favor this artistic genre. This propensity for relief ended by decisively conditioning the art of the Roman urban center, which had by this time been built over almost exclusively with works of court art.

The sculpture of Trajan's Column is closely connected in style to the gigantic frieze later placed on the Arch of Constantine, which was probably originally set in the Forum of Trajan. The hand of a single artist can be seen in both works. He has conventionally been called "The Master of the Feats of Trajan," a title that has also been connected

THE MARVELS OF ROME

But it is now time to pass on to the marvels in building displayed by our own City, and to make some enquiry into the resources and experience that we have gained in the lapse of eight hundred years; and so prove that here, as well, the rest of the world has been outdone by us: a thing which will appear, in fact, to have occurred almost as many times as the marvels are in number which I shall have to enumerate. If, indeed, all the buildings of our City are considered in the aggregate, and supposing them, so to say, all thrown together in one vast mass, the united grandeur of them would lead one to suppose that we were describing another world, accumulated in a single spot.

Not to mention among our great works, the Circus Maximus, that was constructed by the Dictator Caesar, one stadium in width and three in length, and occupying, with the adjacent buildings, no less than four jugera, with room for two hundred and sixty thousand spectators seated; am I not to include in the number of our magnificent constructions, the Basilica of Paulus, with its admirable Phrygian columns; the Forum of the late Emperor Augustus; the Temple of Peace, erected by the Emperor Vespasianus Augustus — some of the finest works that the world has ever beheld — the roofing, too, of the Vote-Office, that was built by Agrippa? not to forget that, before his time, Valerius of Ostia, the architect, had covered in a theatre at Rome, at the time of the public Games celebrated by Libo?

We behold with admiration pyramids that were built by kings, when the very ground alone, that was purchased by the Dictator Caesar, for the construction of his Forum, cost one hundred millions of sesterces! If, too, an enormous expenditure has its attractions for any one whose mind is influenced by monetary considerations, be it known to him that the house in which Clodius dwelt, who was slain by Milo, was purchased by him at the price of fourteen million eight hundred thousand sesterces! a thing that, for my part, I look upon as no less astounding than the monstrous follies that have been displayed by kings.

PLINY THE ELDER:
Natural History (XXXVI:24)

Rome: Forum of Nerva, southeast side. In the center of the Forum there was a temple dedicated to Minerva; above the remaining columns is a frieze depicting myths connected with her cult. The complex, built during Domitian's reign, was inaugurated by Nerva. The rich, baroque style of architectural decoration is typical of the late Flavian Age.

CONSTRUCTION OF THE
PORT OF CIVITAVECCHIA
IN THE TIME OF TRAJAN

This delightful villa is surrounded by the most verdant meadows, and commands a fine view of the sea, which flows into a spacious harbor in the form of an amphitheater. The left-hand of this port is defended by exceeding strong works, and they are now actually employed in carrying out the same on the opposite side. An artificial island, which is rising in the mouth of the harbor, will break the force of the waves and afford a safe channel to ships on each side. In the construction of this wonderful instance of art, stones of a most enormous size are transported hither in a large sort of pontoons, and being piled one upon the other, are fixed by their own weight, and gradually accumulating in the manner of a natural mound. It already lifts its rocky back above the ocean, while the waves which beat upon it, being tossed to an immense height, foam with a prodigious noise and whiten all the sea around. To these stones are added large blocks which, when the whole shall be completed, will give it the appearance of an island just emerged from the ocean. This harbor is to be called by the name of its great founder, Trajan, and will prove of infinite benefit, by affording a very secure retreat to ships on that extensive and dangerous coast. Farewell.

PLINY THE YOUNGER:
Letters to Friends (31)

with the architect of the Forum, Apollodorus of Damascus. Some scholars have recognized the youthful work of this artist in the reliefs on the Arch of Titus, and certain aspects of the art of Trajan's Column are in fact to be found in the earlier work.

The sculpture of Trajan's Column represents a point of fulfillment in Roman art. It had taken centuries to arrive. In the first manifestations of historical relief, such as the *Ara* of Domitius Enobarbus, Greek artistic form had been used in a context imposed by the Romans who commissioned the work, with essentially eclectic results. In the reliefs of Trajan's Column, however, the Hellenistic heritage has been completely absorbed and has fused with elements of plebeian art to form a style perfectly adapted to the realistic and historical content it was called upon to express. The result was basically new, and marked the high point of official Roman art. The scenes on the column unfold one after the other in a continuous ribbon. The sense of historical development, of time uninterrupted in its flow, which connects individual episodes in an almost cinematic way, is achieved without the individual episodes losing any of their individuality . . . This is the first time the continuous relief as an artistic form was realized so consistently.

A comparison with the frozen movement of the procession on the *Ara Pacis*, set in a fixity almost like that of a snapshot, reveals better than any discussion the difference between the classicist Augustan art and Trajanic art. The techniques used to realize the sculpture of the Column range from an exceptionally varied and modulated plastic rendering to sequences that seem to contrast with the realism of the whole, such as the bird's-eye views of cities, their proportions distorted, or the small-scale representation of large objects such as ships. Everything is sustained, however, by the continuous tension that links one scene with another. Far from decreasing this tension, the non-realistic, symbolic, almost stenographic depiction of some scenes accentuates it. It abbreviates the discourse by concentrating only on the essentials.

Yet the values of the humanistic Greek tradition are present here as well, perfectly alive. For example, the Emperor, though set in relief and given his own unmistakable physical characteristics, is not portrayed in a hieratic or hierarchic way; the tendency is rather to depict him in discourse with his officers, in natural positions, a man among men. It is difficult to judge how much propaganda is concealed behind such a conception, but in any case it is propaganda for a public still sensitive to the humanistic aspects of Greek culture. The same mentality is to be seen in the representation of the defeated enemies, killed or taken prisoner. They appear not as ferocious and vile brutes, in the style of later Roman art, but as individuals worthy of respect and understanding. Aeschylus had described the defeated Persians in a similar way.

Decadence in Italy

Unlike the Roman urban center, which is obviously a singular case, the rest of Italy in this period was a spectacle of decadence. The Flavian-Trajanic period was a transition period, but the phenomenon of economic decadence became disastrous and irreversible during the course of the second century. The total disappearance of popular or plebeian art, the principal product of the municipalities during the late Republican and Julian-Claudian period, has already been mentioned. It signaled the collapse of those entrepreneurial classes that had been the backbone of Republican and Augustan Italy.

The process of dissolution can also be seen, though only in its beginning stages, in the cities destroyed by Vesuvius. After the earthquake of A.D. 63, which destroyed a large part of Herculaneum and Pompeii, the cities began an effort of reconstruction, which was not finished when the final destruction took place, in A.D. 79. Besides a

Rome: The markets of Trajan. The grandiose brick exedra that partially conceals the irregular multistoried complex of the shops is one of the best examples of nonofficial urban planning left by ancient Rome.

SOME ARCHITECTURAL PROBLEMS

To the Emperor Trajan

The citizens of Nicea, Sir, are building a theater which, though it is not yet finished, they have already expended, as I am informed (for I have not examined the account myself) above ten million sesterces; and what is worse, I fear, to no purpose. For, either from the foundation being laid on a marshy ground, or that the stones themselves were decayed, the walls are cracked from top to bottom. It deserves your consideration, therefore, whether it would be best to carry on this work or entirely discontinue it; or rather, perhaps, it would not be most prudent absolutely to destroy it, for the foundations upon which this building is raised appear to me more expensive than solid. Several private persons have promised to erect at their own expense, some the portico, others the galleries above the pit; but this design cannot be executed, as the principal fabric is at a standstill.

This city is also rebuilding upon a more enlarged plan the Gymnasium which was burnt down before my arrival in the province. They have already been at some (and, I doubt, a fruitless) expense. The structure is not only irregular and ill-disposed, but the present architect (who, it must be owned, is a rival to the person who was first employed) asserts that the walls, though they are twenty-two feet thick, are not strong enough to support the superstructure, as their interstices are not cemented with mortar, nor are these walls strengthened with a proper covering.

The inhabitants of Claudiopolis are sinking (I cannot call it erecting) a large public bath upon a low spot of ground which lies at the foot of a mountain. The source of the fund appropriated for this work are the admissions paid by those honorary members you were pleased to add to their Senate — at least, they are ready to pay whenever I call upon them. As I am afraid therefore the public money in the city of Nicea and (what is infinitely more valuable than any pecuniary consideration) your benefaction in that of Claudiopolis should be ill applied, I must desire you to send hither an architect to inspect not only the theater but the bath; in order to consider whether, after all the expense which has been laid out, it will be better to finish them upon the present plan, or reform the one and remove the other; for otherwise we may perhaps throw away our future cost, by endeavouring not to lose what we have already expended.

Emperor Trajan to Pliny

You are upon the spot so you will best be able to consider and determine what is proper to be done concerning the theater, which the inhabitants of Nicea are building; as for myself, it will be sufficient if you let me know your determination. With respect to the particular parts of this theater that are to be raised at a private charge, you will see those engagements fulfilled, when the body of the building to which they are to be annexed shall be finished. These paltry Greeks are, I know, immoderately fond of gymnastic diversions and therefore, perhaps, the citizens of Nicea have planned a more magnificent fabric for this purpose than is necessary; however, they must be contented with such as will be sufficient to answer the use for which it is intended. I entirely leave to you to advise the citizens of Claudiopolis as you shall think proper, with relation to their bath, which they have placed it seems in a very improper situation. As there is no province that is not furnished with men of skill and ingenuity, you cannot possibly want for architects; unless you think it the shortest way to procure them from Rome, when it is generally from Greece that they come to us.

PLINY THE YOUNGER:
Correspondence with Trajan (48-49)

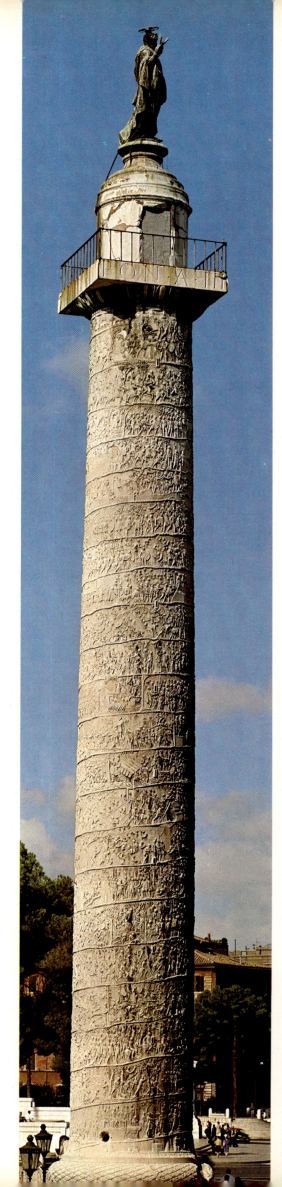

Rome: Trajan's Column. Inaugurated in A.D. 113, the column is close to 125 feet high, with its base; the column alone is 100 feet tall. In the base, decorated with friezes of arms and festoons held up by eagles, is the cella where Trajan's ashes were placed. The famous frieze representing the two Dacian wars is sculptured around the column and is almost 125 yards long. Inside the column a spiral staircase was cut out; this leads to the small terrace formed by the abacus of the capital. The statue of the emperor was placed on the top. It disappeared in the Middle Ages and in 1587 Pope Sixtus V replaced it with a statue of St. Peter.

INSCRIPTION ON THE TRAJAN COLUMN

The Senate and the People of Rome to the Emperor, Caesar Nerva, son of the deified Nerva, Traianus Augustus, Germanicus, Dacicus, Pontifex Maximus, etc., etc., to demonstrate how lofty a hill and what area of ground was carried away for these mighty works.

general decline in quality in the new work — in wall-painting, for example — which corresponds to a considerable cultural decadence, the decline of some of the most remarkable houses and villas of the preceding period is worthy of mention. The "Cryptoporticus House" at Pompeii and the House of the Samnite in Herculaneum were occupied by new owners, who broke them up into small apartments. The case of the Villa of Mysteries is particularly impressive; from a luxury residence it became a rustic villa, its refined rooms used for rough agricultural functions. This was the case with almost all the villas in the Pompeian territory in the period between Nero and the Flavians. In the *Satyricon* of Petronius, written during Nero's reign, the guests at Trimalchio's dinner deplore the economic deterioration of the city where the scene takes place; a port town in Campania, almost certainly to be identified with Pozzuoli. At that period, the crisis was only beginning, however; conditions were to grow worse and worse.

There is no lack of phenomena that seem to contradict this general decadence, of course. The most striking can be seen at Herculaneum,

Rome: Reliefs from Trajan's Column. Opposite page (119): From the bottom up the scenes depict: 1 Construction of a camp; bound Dacian prisoners; wounded Roman soldiers being treated; the departure of the army; a prisoner is presented to the emperor. 2. Trajan, near the Danube, receives two submissive barbarian chiefs; the army passes over the Danube on a bridge of boats. 3. Trajan's speech to the soldiers; forest trees being felled; the heads of two Dacians placed on spears are displayed before the fortifications. 4. Trajan, on a hill, watches an attack of the Numidian cavalry.

Left: from the bottom up.

1. Construction of a camp; the camp is built; the cavalry passes over a wooden bridge. 2. The Dacians in flight; the Romans wade through a river; Trajan receives the Dacian ambassadors. 3. The Roman army, in a city on the Danube, prepares for a new expedition; the army passes over the river on a variety of boats with their horses and provisions.

Right:

Above: Detail from one of the two *Anaglypha Trajani* (marble relief panels) in the Forum of Trajan. The emperor giving a speech from the Julian rostra. In the background the Arch of Augustus and the Temple of Castor and Pollux are visible.

Below: Another detail from the reliefs of the two *Anaglypha Trajani*. (The Curia of the Roman Forum, Rome.)

Rome: Relief from the Temple of Hadrian,
with a representation of a province. (Palazzo
dei Conservatori, Rome.)

THE PLEASURES OF THE TUSCAN
VILLA OF PLINY THE YOUNGER

The villa sits on the slope of a hill but has a view as from the very top... At the extremity of a portico stands a grand dining room, which opens upon one end of the terrace; from the windows there is an extensive prospect over the meadows up into the countryside, from whence you also have a view of the terrace and such parts of the house that project forward, together with the woods enclosing the adjacent hippodrome (or circular walk). Opposite almost to the center of the portico stands a square edifice that encompasses a small area shaded by four plane trees in the midst of which a fountain rises, from whence the water running over the edges of the marble basin gently refreshes the surrounding plane trees and the verdure underneath them. This apartment consists of a bed-chamber secured from every kind of noise and which the light itself cannot penetrate; together with the dining room that I use when I have none but intimate friends with me.

A second portico looks upon this little area and has the same prospect as the former just described. There is, besides, another room, which being situated close to the nearest plane tree, enjoys a constant shade and verdure; its sides are encrusted half-way with carved marble; and from thence to the ceiling a foliage is painted with birds intermixed among the branches, which has an effect altogether agreeable as that of the carving; at the base of a little fountain, playing through several small pipes into a vase, the water produces a most pleasing murmur. From a corner of this portico you enter into a very spacious chamber opposite to the grand dining room, which from some of its windows has a view of the terrace and from others of the meadow; those in the front look upon a cascade, which entertains both the eye and the ear, for the water dashing from a great height foams over the marble basin that receives it from below. This room is extremely warm in winter, being much exposed to the sun; and in a cloudy day the heat of an adjoining stove very well supplies its absence.

From thence you pass through a spacious and pleasant undressing room into the cold-bath room, in which is a large, gloomy bath; but if you are disposed to swim more at large or in warmer water, in the middle of the area is a wide basin for the purpose, and near it a reservoir from whence you may be supplied with cold water to brace yourself again, if you should perceive you are too much relaxed by the warm water. Contiguous to the cold bath is another of a moderate degree of heat, which enjoys the kindly warmth of the sun but not so intensely as that of the hot bath, which projects further....

But not to dwell any longer upon this digression, lest I should myself be condemned by the maxim I have just laid down, I have now informed you why I prefer my Tuscan villa to those that I possess at Tusculum, Tiber, and Praeneste. Besides the advantages already mentioned, I here enjoy a more profound retirement, as I am at the farther distance from the business of the town and the interruptions of troublesome avocations. All is calm and composed, circumstances that contribute, no less than its clear air and unclouded sky, to that health of body and cheerfulness of mind that I particularly enjoy in this place, both of which I preserve by the exercise of study and hunting. Indeed, there is no place that agrees better with all my family in general, as I am sure, at least, that I have not yet lost one (and I speak it with the sentiments I ought) of all those I brought with me hither. May the gods continue their happiness to me and that honor to my villa. Farewell!

PLINY THE YOUNGER:
Correspondence (V:6)

where the neighborhoods near the sea were partly rebuilt in the period between the earthquake and the eruption. This is the continuation of a process already begun during the Julian-Claudian age, when many pieces of property were combined, and the splendid houses looking over the sea were created: the "House of the Deer," the "House of the Mosaic Atrium," the "House of the Reliefs of Telephus," which recent excavations have brought to light. Construction at Herculaneum was only an apparent exception to the decadence, however. Unlike Pompeii, which was always a large commercial, industrial, and agricultural center, Herculaneum during the Imperial Age was a little resort town, frequented by rich Romans, and felt the effects of upheavals in the local economy much less. The very fact that it was possible to buy up various houses in order to create larger complexes is proof of the economic crisis within the local ruling class, which surrendered its place not so much to a class of "nouveaux riches," as had occurred many times in the past, but rather to individuals from the urban areas, whose wealth did not depend (or depended only to a small degree) on the prosperity of the local economy and was based above all on the possession of large estates: Pliny the Elder, and his nephew and adopted son, Pliny the Younger, are examples of this sort of person. Among other things, their writings furnish a rare picture of the economic and social situation of the period.

The Empire Under Hadrian

If Trajan represented the new Caesar, the soldier-prince, the propagator of an extensive Empire, Hadrian consciously attempted to be the new Augustus, organizer and arranger of the state structure from every point of view — administrative, economic, and cultural. This ideological link with the personality of the first emperor is to be seen even in facts that look insignificant at first glance. It was Hadrian, for instance, who restored many Augustan monuments, such as the Forum of Augustus and the Pantheon; Trajan had concerned himself with Caesar's urban projects.

The period that began with Hadrian and ended with Commodus was on the whole the most prosperous through which the Empire passed. The economy of the provinces greatly expanded in this period; production and trade reached levels unsurpassed until the modern age. Roman ships now normally included ports in the Persian Gulf and the Indian Ocean in their itineraries, and products from India and China flowed into the Mediterranean area. At the same time, urban civilization reached its peak. With provinces that were almost separate nations, the Empire was no longer a political-administrative fact based on the superior military of one city-state, Rome; it was an association of cities, all with considerable autonomy, gathered together predominantly for administrative convenience. Its unity was based on the economic, social, and cultural achievements of urban life, which were common to all the provinces, western and eastern.

In this framework, Italy was an element all to itself. Largely depopulated, economically parasitical, it was by this time a mere accumulation of senatorial landed estates, which to a certain extent prefigured the later feudal structure. The case was different with Rome and the minor centers functionally connected to her, however, such as Ostia and the city of Portus, which grew up around the new port of call founded by Claudius and enlarged by Trajan. The capital was now totally divorced from its old hinterland, which could no longer support her. Rome became more than ever an expression of the sheer pomp and apparatus of Empire, a backdrop for official shows, a stage for official court art and culture. Great masses of people thronged around the monumental center, feeding at the state's expense or devoted to the tertiary service industries of the capital. The urban problems that arose from the need to house this enormous mass — perhaps a million people — was resolved by the creation of multi-story apartment buildings, or *insulae*, whose modernity is thoroughly amazing. Examples of these buildings are to be found at Rome, although the best surviving examples are at Ostia Antica.

The first two emperors of the second century, not so incidentally, Trajan and Hadrian, were both provincial in origin; they were Spanish. During the same period, the olive oil used in Rome and in most of Italy came almost exclusively from Spain. Before it was excavated, there existed near the Tiber Market an entire artificial hill, formed of an incalculable number of Spanish oil amphorae — their brand names and other inscriptions proving them such.

Building activity in Rome was at its peak during Hadrian's reign, and from this period forward regulation of building by the state authority became customary. Setting the consular date on the brick seals that served as brand names had been commonly done from Trajan's time, but in Hadrian's time the use of the date with the seal became obligatory. This may have taken place in A.D. 123, which would explain the great number of seals for that year that have been preserved. The decisive intervention by the state in the most important existing industry in Rome, building construction, can be followed by means of these brick seals. Little by little the furnaces, kilns, and quarries, once the property of private individuals, seem to have passed into the hands of the Emperor, who thus found himself in an ideal situation for instituting a policy of low-cost public building.

Art in the Reign of Hadrian: The Pantheon

The most representative monument of Hadrian's period is probably the Pantheon. Examination of the brick seals has demonstrated that the building is not the edifice built by Agrippa in 27 B.C., but a new construction that can be dated at the beginning of Hadrian's reign, between A.D. 118 and 128. The marvelous technical achievement of this building, one of the most remarkable in ancient architecture, is never an end in itself, but corresponds perfectly to the function the building was intended to serve. The form and technique of construction bear as well a symbolic weight whose meaning is quite clear.

The cupola of the Pantheon is the largest ever built with traditional means — that is, before the introduction of reinforced concrete. Its diameter, 142-$\frac{1}{2}$ feet, is slightly larger than that of the cupola of St. Peter's. The entire building is based on a system of remarkably simplified relationships. Its height is the same as the diameter of the cupola, and the interior consists of a cylinder surmounted by a semi-sphere whose radius corresponds to the height of the cylinder. Monumentality and solemnity are the result of this simple relationship, and though the building is articulated in a series of rather complex subdivisions, they are not detrimental to its unity. On the contrary, they emphasize the axes and focal points of a space that would otherwise seem undifferentiated and thus devoid of sense. These articulations are not merely technical in their function, either, but correspond to symbolic motifs and cult practices, as does the edifice in its entirety.

The Pantheon, as its name reveals, was dedicated to "all the gods" of the celestial pantheon. The cupola symbolizes — in the clearest possible manner — the vault of the heavens, while its great central opening, which is, with the entranceway, the only source of light, corresponds to the sun. This relationship must have been even more evident in ancient times if, as is probable, there were ornamental stars at the center of the coffers that decorate the cupola. The arrangement of the niches and the shrines, in correspondence with the axes oriented according to the cardinal points of the compass, shows that the statues of the gods were placed at the precise points dictated by ancient augural discipline, so that the terrestrial temple, with its circular plan and cupola, became a faithful projection of the celestial panoply.

From a structural point of view, the edifice is the most remarkable achievement of vaulted Roman architecture; through the methods used in it, the construction of huge internal spaces ceased to be a problem. From the end of the second century on, the premises of this architecture became more and more firmly rooted.

Yet the problem of the relationship between interior and exterior space does not seem to be solved. The facade is a huge octastyle portico surmounted by a pediment, which keeps fully to Greek tradition. This was even more evident at that time, when the edifice rose up from a stairway and behind a long axial portico. This frontal arrangement, the only one then considered appropriate, rendered the cylinder and most of the cupola practically invisible. The temple thus had a completely traditional aspect, which was perhaps necessary to make its function immediately recognizable. The exterior and interior space were completely independent and had no relation to each other. With the elevation of the ground (it has now covered the stairway) and the disappearance of the front portico and the other edifices that once surrounded the Pantheon, the original relationship of the portico to the circular portion of the building has been lost. In the more complete view now possible, the contrast between the front portico and the cylinder with its cupola can be seen quite easily. The problem of their relationship to each other has existed from the beginning, of course, and was originally solved only by the separation of the two views.

IN PRAISE OF THE ROMAN EMPIRE

For it is she (Rome) who first proved that oratory cannot reach every goal. About her not only is it impossible to speak properly, but it is impossible even to see her properly. . . . For beholding so many hills occupied by buildings, or on plains so many meadows completely urbanized, or so much land brought under the name of one city, who could survey her accurately? And from what point of observation?

Homer says of snow that, as it falls, it covers "the crest of the range and the mountain peaks and the flowering fields and the rich acres of men, and," he says, "it is poured out over the white sea, the harbors and the shores." So also of this city. Like the snow, she covers mountain peaks, she covers the land intervening, and she goes down to the sea, where the commerce of all mankind has its common exchange and all the produce of the earth has its common market. Wherever one may go in Rome, there is no vacancy to keep one from being, there also, in midcity. And indeed she is poured out, not just over the level ground, but in a manner with which the simile cannot begin to keep pace, she rises great distances into the air, so that her height is not to be compared to a covering of snow but rather to the peaks themselves. And as a man who far surpasses others in size and strength likes to show his strength by carrying others on his back, so this city, which is built over so much land, is not satisfied with her extent, but raising upon her shoulders others of equal size, one over the other, she carries them. It is from this that she gets her name, and strength (rômé) is the mark of all that is hers. Therefore, if one chose to unfold, as it were, and lay flat on the ground the cities which now she carries high in air, and place them side by side, all that part of Italy which intervenes would, I think, be filled and become one continuous city stretching to the Strait of Otranto.

Though she is so vast as perhaps even now I have not sufficiently shown, but as the eye attests more clearly, it is not possible to say of her as of other cities, 'There she stands'. Again it has been said of the capital cities of the Athenians and the Lacedaemonians — and may no ill omen attend the comparison — — that the first would in size appear twice as great as in its intrinsic power, the second far inferior in size to its intrinsic power. . . . this city is to the boundaries and territory of the entire civilized world, as if the latter were a country district and she had been appointed the common town. It might be said that this one citadel is the refuge and assembly place of all *perioeci* or of all who dwell in outside demes.

She has never failed them, but like the soil of the earth, she supports all men; and as the sea, which receives with its gulfs all the many rivers, hides them and holds them all and still, with what goes in and out, is and seems ever the same, so actually this city receives those who flow in from all the earth and has even sameness in common with the sea. The latter is not made greater by the influx of rivers, for it has been ordained by fate that with the waters flowing in, the sea maintain its volume; here no change is visible because the city is so great.

But of this city, great in every respect, no one could say that she has not created power in keeping with her magnitude. No, if one looks at the whole empire and reflects how small a fraction rules the whole world, he may be amazed at the city, but when he has beheld the city herself and the boundaries of the city, he can no longer be amazed that the entire civilized world is ruled by one so great.

AELIUS ARISTIDES:
In gloria di Roma (6–9, 61–62)

Just before his death, he compelled Servianus, then ninety years old, to kill himself, as has been said before, in order that Servianus might not outlive him, and, as he thought, become emperor. He likewise gave orders that very many others who were guilty of slight offences should be put to death; these, however, were spared by Antoninus. And he is said, as he lay dying, to have composed the following lines:

"O blithe little soul, thou, flitting away,
Guest and comrade of this my clay,
Whither now goest thou, to what place
Bare and ghastly and without grace?
Nor, as thy wont was, joke and play."

Such verses as these did he compose, and not many that were better, and also some in Greek.

He lived 62 years, 5 months, 17 days. He ruled 20 years, 11 months.

Scriptores Historiae Augustae (XXV-XXVI)

Rome: Section and plan of the Pantheon (A.D. 118-128).

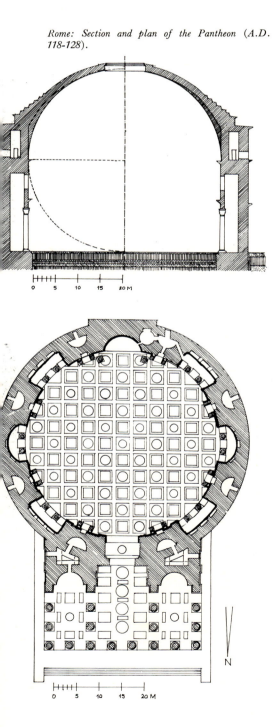

From its Augustan origins, the Pantheon had borne a precise dynastic meaning. It glorified the ancestors of the Giulia family who were associated with the gods of the sky, the planets, and the stars. Venus, who was one of them, was considered the family's first progenitor. It is interesting to note that one of the first edifices restored by Hadrian was exactly that one that best corresponded to his political, religious, and dynastic program. Even more than Augustus, Hadrian emphasized the interrelationship between the cosmos (dominion of the gods), and the Roman Empire which represented the immutable order of the earth — the political system which was the dominion of the prince. For an idea of the ideological form the Imperial power definitively assumed from Hadrian on, there is no better text than the Pantheon.

Such a high-level program of centralization and universalization was naturally reflected in every aspect of Roman art, at least in urban and court art. Like Augustus, but with the greater consistency and profundity afforded him by the new political and social situation, Hadrian imposed a precise cultural program that once again found its natural expression in classicism. Hadrian's was a classicism less rigorous than Augustus', however, less connected to neo-Attic art, even though classical Athens was always the fundamental reference point. (The importance of Hadrian's building program in the glorious ancient city is well-known.) Artistic expressions of Hellenistic derivation were allowed, nor was pharaonic Egypt excluded, even though Hadrian detested turbulent Alexandria, in which he saw the very essence of everything adverse to his program of ordered, Olympian autocracy.

It is hardly fortuitous that, among the few historic sculptured reliefs of Hadrian's Age that have come down to us, static scenes of presentation, sacrifice, or apotheosis prevail. The pacific Hadrian would not have himself depicted in warlike poses, for that matter. Of particular significance are the splendid *tondi* (round panels) later inserted in the Arch of Constantine, in which the emperor is depicted hunting wild beasts and sacrificing to divinities connected with the hunt. It was an old Near Eastern idea, later taken up by the Hellenistic princes, that the only activity worthy of a sovereign in times of peace was hunting. For Rome, the example had been set by Scipio Emilianus. A sympathetic Polybius describes him as deserting the activities of the Roman Forum in order to give himself up to the pleasures of hunting in the Pontine plain. Such pleasures may seem gratuitous, and their depiction a whim of decoration, but in the light of the ideological preoccupation of Roman art, a sculpture of Hadrian hunting shows a certain amount of thoughtful "programming."

Hadrian's Villa at Tivoli

Hadrian's nature and his tendencies could no longer, given the structure of Roman polity, be purely private matters. They became, in fact, more and more a part of his public function. Their most obvious expression is to be found in the elaborate villa Hadrian had built a short distance from Tivoli. Unlike Augustus, who for political reasons liked to accentuate his bourgeois origins and tastes, Hadrian wanted to erect a "screen" between himself and the court, and between the court and the tumultuous and chaotic city. The function of Hadrian's villa, like the palace and its park at Versailles, was to place the emperor outside and beyond the sphere of common men, in an abstract space that made veneration easier. The difference from the policy of the preceding emperor was sharp. Trajan loved to have himself depicted among his soldiers and the masses, a man among men, although this may have been a pose, manufactured for political reasons. To a certain degree the portraits of Trajan hark back to the tradition of Republican realism. With Hadrian, the Imperial portrait takes on a more official, formal aspect, and is dressed in idealized and classical forms.

He built public buildings in all places and without number, but he inscribed his own name on none of them except the temple of his father Trajan. At Rome he restored the Pantheon, the Voting-enclosure, the Basilica of Neptune, very many temples, the Forum of Augustus, the Baths of Agrippa, and dedicated all of them in the names of their original builders. Also he constructed the bridge named after himself, a tomb on the bank of the Tiber, and the temple of the Bona Dea. With the aid of the architect Decrianus he raised the Colossus and, keeping it in an upright position, moved it away from the place in which the Temple of Rome is now, though its weight was so vast that he had to furnish for the work as many as twenty-four elephants.

Scriptores Historiae Augustae (XIX)

Despite its large proportions, Hadrian's Villa is not so far removed in its conception from other Roman villas. It was not a palace with an attached park (such as has prevailed in the modern age, beginning with the Renaissance) but rather a series of pavilions immersed in nature, built with a variety and complexity that fit them to the natural lines of the terrain. The buildings were not even set in one line, but rather along four principal axes made necessary by the shape of the land and of varying length, from 205 feet to 377 feet. It was not built all at once. Rather it "grew" as its various parts were conceived and realized in succeeding ages. This is again demonstrated by the brick seals: those in the villa cover practically all of Hadrian's reign, from A.D. 117 to 138.

The individual structures were as varied as the plan. Among the buildings of the villa a series of new and bold structural techniques created continual surprises. The methods of covering space that were used — vaults, semi-cupolas and cupolas — formed unpredictable spaces and prospects, and the rigid axiality typical of Roman architecture was tempered by the use of complex building plans in which bilateral symmetry gave way to richer and more dynamic solutions. It is no wonder that baroque architects, Borromini in particular, were attracted by the buildings of the villa, which they drew many times

Left and below:
Rome: The Pantheon, interior and exterior. The inscription of Agrippa, part of the original building, was reproduced by Hadrian and placed on the newly built temple.

Following pages:
Rome: *Tondi* (round panels) from the age of Hadrian, used in the Arch of Constantine. That on the left depicts a boar-hunting scene; that on the right, a sacrifice to Diana.

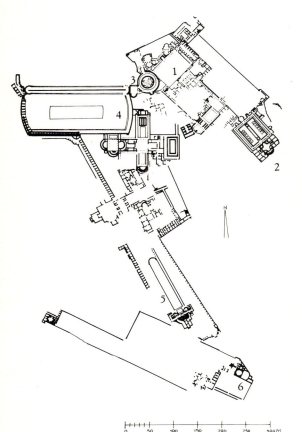

Tivoli: Schematic drawing of Hadrian's Villa (A.D.118-134).
1 *Courtyard of the Libraries*
2 *Piazza d'Oro (Golden Square)*
3 *Maritime Theater*
4 *The Poekile, a colonnaded area*
5 *Canopus*
6 *Academy*

Tivoli: Hadrian's Villa. Overall view of the Canopus. The *Historia Augusta* records that Hadrian built reproductions of the monuments he most admired during his travels. This long basin seems to represent the canal of Canopus, which linked Alexandria with the Temple of Serapis at Canopus. The building on the left, at the end of the canal, a triclinium, has the same plan as the temple of Isis in Rome. Recent excavations have uncovered sculptures clearly connected with Egypt, as well as copies of Attic sculpture of the fifth century B.C.

Left:
Tivoli: Hadrian's Villa. Detail from the curved side of the Canopus, with reproductions of the Phidian Amazon and a Mars, Greek works of the fifth century B.C. (These are cement casts; the original copies are in a small museum nearby.)

Right:
Tivoli: Hadrian's Villa. The so-called Maritime Theater. In reality this is a small round islet, occupied by a series of small rooms and surrounded by a canal and a colonnaded portico. Originally only two wooden drawbridges connected the central complex with the rest of the villa; it could thus be totally isolated. Assumed to be the private refuge of the emperor, its exact function is still to be explained.

Tivoli: Hadrian's Villa. Detail of the preceding plan.
1 Small Thermae
2 Great Thermae
3 Vestibule
4 Canopus

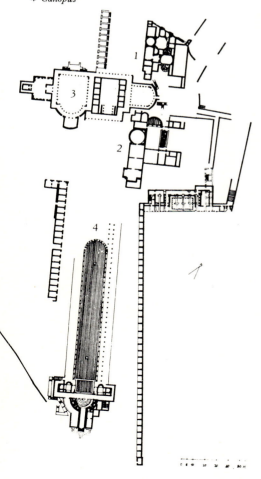

and from which they certainly obtained considerable inspiration. The Piazza d'Oro, the Small Baths and the Maritime Theater move quite decisively outside the usual schemes of ancient architecture to anticipate modern forms.

It has often been said that the emperor himself was the architect of the villa. Hadrian loved to pose as an artist, and he did cultivate almost all the arts, from painting to architecture to poetry. It is most improbable, however, that he had the technical knowledge necessary for the realization of a work that is considered among the most remarkable in ancient architecture. It is certain, though, that the emperor, who had commissioned the work, imposed his point of view regarding the planning of the whole, and some of the elements, such as the Maritime Theater, seem too close to an intimate, personal vision, to be independent of the will and choice of Hadrian himself. This circular islet, ringed by a canal, could be completely isolated by removing two drawbridges. It displays in the clearest possible way the desire of the person who conceived it to isolate himself in the very heart of the

Rome: The Temple of Antoninus and Faustina in the Forum. Erected by the Emperor in honor of his deified wife after her death in A.D. 141, it was later dedicated to the Emperor as well after his death in A.D. 161. (His name was added to the upper part of the architrave, the lower part of which bore his wife's name.) In the Middle Ages the Temple was transformed into a church, San Lorenzo in Miranda. On the columns, monoliths of Cipollian marble, the grooves that are visible were made by ropes used in the vain attempt to demolish the columns and use the material in other constructions.

A VIEW OF LIFE IN ROME AT THE BEGINNING OF THE SECOND CENTURY A.D.

At Rome 'tis worse; where house-rent by the
    year,
And servants' bellies cost so devilish dear;
And tavern bills run high for hungry cheer.
To drink or eat in earthernware we scorn,
Which cheaply country cupboards does
    adorn:
And coarse blue hoods on holidays are worn.
Some distant parts of Italy are known,
Where none but only dead men wear a gown
But here, attired beyond our purse we go,
For useless ornament and flaunting show:
We take on trust, in purple robes to shine:
And poor are yet ambitious to be fine.
This is a common vice, though all things
    here
Are sold, and sold unconscionably dear.
Who fears in country towns a house's fall,
Or to be caught betwixt a riven wall?
But we inhabit a weak city here;
Which buttresses and props but scarcely bear:
And 'tis the village mason's daily calling,
To keep the world's metropolis from falling,
To cleanse the gutters, and the chinks to close;
And, for one night, secure his lord's repose.
At Cumae we can sleep quite round the year,
Nor falls, nor fires, nor nightly dangers fear:
While rolling flames from Roman turrets fly,
And the pale citizens for buckets cry.
Thy neighbour has removed his wretched store
(Few hands will rid the lumber of the poor);
Thy own third story smokes, while thou,
    supine,
Art drench'd in fumes of undigested wine.
For if the lowest floors already burn,
Cocklofts and garrets soon will take the turn;
Where thy tame pigeons next the tiles were
    bred,
Which, in their nests unsafe, are timely fled.
'Tis frequent here, for want of sleep, to die;
Which fumes of undigested feasts deny;
And, with imperfect heat, in languid stomachs
    fry.
What house secure from noise the poor can
    keep,
When e'en the rich can scarce afford to sleep:
So dear it costs to purchase rest in Rome;
And hence the sources of diseases come.
The drover who his fellow drover meets
In narrow passages of winding streets;
The wagoners that curse their standing teams,
Would wake e'en drowsy Drusius from his
    dreams.
And yet the wealthy will not brook delay,
But sweep above our heads, and make their
    way:
In lofty litters borne, and read and write,
Or sleep at ease: the shutters make it night.
    Return we to the dangers of the night:
And first behold our houses' dreadful height;
From whence come broken potsherds tumbling
    down;
And leaky ware from garret windows thrown:
Well may they break our heads, that mark the
    flinty stone.
'Tis want of sense to sup abroad too late;
Unless thou first hast settled thy estate.
As many fates attend thy steps to meet
As there are waking windows in the street,
Bless the good gods, and think thy chance is
    rare
To have a pisspot only for thy share.

JUVENAL: *Third Satire*

residence, to detach himself from the cares and tasks that the administration of the Empire continuously thrust upon him. The romantic "Hadrianic" poetry that has survived speaks to the same feeling, the same need for isolation.

Besides such cases as the Maritime Theater, directly linked to what is known of his personality, the intervention of the emperor in the conception of the villa may be seen and proved not so much from the technical point of view as through the ideological meaning each building bears in its context. According to a fourth century historian, the villa consists of reproductions of the most famous monuments admired by Hadrian during his journeys to the provinces. While there is no reason to suspect this information, the value and limits of the concept of imitation should be understood. All the structures of Hadrian's villa correspond perfectly to architectural styles of the second century A.D. If imitation was attempted, then, it was more likely "free" imitation, more allusive than realistic. It is really almost impossible to imagine the concept of an "architectural copy" in this period. Within these limits, however, the historian's statement is quite interesting. It seems appropriate that Hadrian should wish to surround himself with buildings that were in a certain sense representative and symbolic of the provinces of the Empire. The villa thus became a sort of microcosm, the sum and synthesis of the "Romanized" universe, and the Emperor imposed himself in the clearest and most explicit manner as the center and keystone of the whole system. A conception of this kind corresponds rather well to everything that is known about Hadrian's personality and political outlook.

Art and Society Under the Antonines: The Column of Marcus Aurelius

Antoninus Pius was distinguished from his predecessor by his much more modest, "bourgeois" qualities, but by the time he came to rule, Hadrian's imprint on the Empire was definitive. His policy was to be followed consistently for many decades. The temple to the deified Hadrian that Antoninus erected, whose northern colonnade still stands (and is one side of the modern building housing the Stock Exchange, in Piazza di Pietra) is highly interesting from several points of view. Just as in the case of the temple erected by Hadrian for his predecessor, north of the Forum of Trajan, the temple in Piazza di Pietra completes and is connected to a series of edifices built by Hadrian: the temple dedicated to his mother-in-law Matidia and the basilicas of Matidia and Marciana. Considerable dynastic continuity is implied by all of this. The fact was that every emperor already foresaw his deification. Almost all the emperors began urban plans during their lifetime, and these were meant to be completed only after their death by the erection of a sanctuary for the new "god."

The sculpture that decorates the interior of the cella of Hadrian's Temple consists of a series of female figures that symbolize the provinces of the Empire holding trophies. At the same time, Antoninus Pius had a series of coins struck that bear personifications of the provinces on one side. After all that has been said about Hadrian's organizing activities and his interest in the administration of the Empire, (and in this regard as well, Antonius followed his predecessor), it is almost superfluous to emphasize the obvious political meaning of these figures. What can usefully be pointed out is the drier, more rigid, and more archaistic style into which Hadrian's classicism — so very vital and replete with Hellenistic moods — was transformed by the age that followed his. The tendency of the age of Antoninus Pius, who came from the upper ranks of the state bureaucracy, was to reassert the value of all the aspects of more ancient Roman and Italic tradition. The process had its sources in the policies of Augustus, of course, but the resuscitation of an already dead world, like the cold classicism that was its formal dress, survived Antoninus Pius for only a few years, and finally gave way to completely opposite artistic and ideological forms.

Already with Marcus Aurelius (A.D. 161–180) the change had begun. Antonine classicism is very vivid, as we can see in the portraits of this emperor and even more in those of Lucius Verus, who shared with him in the rule of the Empire. But it was above all in the age of Commodus (A.D. 180–192), Marcus Aurelius' degenerate son, that the break with classical form took place. It is certainly no accident that during this time, between the end of the second century and the first years of the third, there grew up the profound economic, political, and social crises that shook the foundations of the Empire. It managed to survive only through the total reconstruction and reorganization begun by Diocletian and finished by Constantine and the other emperors of the fourth century.

It was in the reign of Marcus Aurelius that the movement of the Germanic and Sarmatian populations began. The depredations of these groups were to be among the decisive causes of the collapse of Roman power. The Quadi and the Marcomanni actually penetrated into Italy, something that had not occurred for centuries, and the emperor had to take over command of the army himself to resist them. At the same time, a terrible pestilence spread over the land; it caused Aurelius' death in the plains of Vienna. The presentiment of "decline and fall" that such events provoked is clearly present in the spiritual diary of the emperor, written in Greek. In this work the pessimistic outlook of the emperor goes so far that he doubts the validity of his own office; only his characteristic tenacious sense of duty and responsibility allows him to go on with the task entrusted to him. Some parts of his diary demonstrate how far the critical outlook pervaded even the most acute spirits. Particularly remarkable is the passage in which, taking up and accepting the pirate's famous reply to Alexander the Great, the emperor compares the Roman legionary to the brigand. Although the emperor's judgment was a purely private one, not meant to be divulged, it was nevertheless a symptom of the withering away of trust in the Empire's ideological foundations.

The monument that best renders this historic moment is the Column of Marcus Aurelius, erected after his death by his son Commodus. Clearly inspired by Trajan's Column, it differs in some minor details — the base is taller and there are a smaller number of coils, which makes the figures taller. More important, however, is the fact that the relief is much more deeply cut, and shows the taste of the age for violent and dramatic contrasts of light and dark. The harsh technique also renders the scenes more legible. The Hellenistic fluidity that was one of the main characteristics of Trajan's Column, here gives way to a broken and staccato vision. The figures, less numerous and more bulky, are rendered in much greater definition; natural backgrounds are extremely simplified or almost nonexistent; standardized pictorial schemes are insistently repeated; the recurring figures of the emperor and those near him are almost always facing totally to the front. (All these motifs anticipate the "Late Ancient" artistic style). In the Column of Marcus Aurelius, expression has become more important than form, and the equilibrium between these two fundamental aspects of every artistic work has been thoroughly upset. The result is a tense, dramatic art that tends to accentuate the inhuman and horrible aspects of war. The massacre of prisoners, decapitations, the deportation of women and children, are repeated constantly; the faces of the barbarians (and those of the Romans also) are contorted and deformed by painful and grotesque expressions. The drill has here become the sculptor's fundamental tool. Unlike the chisel, which graduates surfaces and thus accentuates the organic, fluid aspects of relief, the drill makes deep cuts and creates dark areas next to completely vivid light ones. The vision rendered is more or less plastic, but it replaces a rational element with an irrational one. This fragmented, detached form was obviously most efficacious and fit for a society in crisis, stricken by the presentiment of its decadence.

TWO THOUGHTS BY MARCUS AURELIUS

From some high place as it were to looke downe, and to behold here flocks, and there sacrifices, without number; and all kinde of navigation; some in a ruffe and stormie sea, and some in a calme: the general differences, or different estates of things, some, that are now first upon being; the severall and mutuall relations of those things that are together; and some other things that are at their last. Their lives also, who were long agoe, and theirs who shall be hereafter, and the present estate and life of those many nations of Barbarians that are now in the world, thou must likewise consider in thy minde. And how many there be, who never so much as heard of thy Name, how many that will soone forget it; how many who but even now did commend thee, within a very little while perchance will speake ill of thee. So that neither fame, nor honour, nor any thing else that this world doth afford, is worth the while.

Meditations (**XXIX**)

As the Spider, when it hath caught the Fly that it hunted after, is not little proud, nor meanely conceited of her selfe: as hee likewise that hath caught an Hare, or hath taken a Fish with his net: as another for the taking of a Boare, and another of a Beare: so may they be proud, and applaud themselves for their valiant acts against the Sarmatae, or Northern Nations lately defeated. For these also, these famous souldiers and warlike men, if thou dost looke into their mindes and opinions, what doe they for the most part but hunt after prey?

Meditations (**X**)

Left:
Rome: The Column of Marcus Aurelius. Standing in present-day Piazza Colonna, it was erected by Commodus in honor of his father, and finished in A.D. 193. Like its twin, the Column of Trajan, it is some 100 feet high without its base. The spiral frieze depicts the wars against the Quadi and the Marcomanni. A statue of Marcus Aurelius once stood at the top of the column; Pope Sixtus V replaced it with a statue of St. Paul in 1589, as a complement to the statue of St. Peter on Trajan's Column.

Right:
Rome: The Column of Marcus Aurelius. Detail. The relief is higher and deeper cut, and the figures larger, than on the Column of Trajan.

Outskirts of Rome: Sant'Urbano alla Caffarella. This medieval church occupies a small second-century A.D. temple built entirely in brick except for the columns of the facade. The building may have been a part of Herodes Atticus' villa (the *Pago Triopio*) which lay in this area, between the third and seventh mile of the Appian Way; or possibly it was the Temple of Demeter and Faustina.

Below:
Santa Maria Capua Vetere (ancient Capua): The Campanian Amphitheater. This building of the age of Hadrian is the largest amphitheater remaining, after the Colosseum. Its axes are 548 feet by 450 feet. The exterior is rather similar to its Roman counterpart, with three superimposed orders and an attic; another similar element is the construction of underground rooms beneath the arena. The decoration of the keystones with the heads of gods is remarkable.

Outskirts of Rome: The so-called Tomb of Annia Regilla. This lovely brick sepulcher, built in the second century A.D., lies near the Appian Way in the Caffarella valley. Its strange position excludes any possible relation with the *Pago Triopio*. (Annia Regilla, the wife of Herodes Atticus, was actually buried in Greece.)

Private Art in the Second Century

Just as in the official sphere, in the private sphere the second century was a period of profound transformations. After Hadrian's Villa there rose in the suburbs of Rome imposing villas that even today, together with the aqueducts and sepulchers, are among the greatest attractions in the Roman Campagna. One of the most grandiose villas was the *Pago Triopio* of Herodes Atticus, a wealthy banker who lived in the period between Hadrian and Marcus Aurelius, which was built between the third and seventh mile of the Appian Way. Among the few remains of this immense property, one of the most notable is the little temple dating from Marcus Aurelius' time (now the church of Sant'Urbano alla Caffarella), which some investigators think may have been a sanctuary dedicated to Demeter and to Faustina. This building is characterized by extensive use of brick; the entire structure is made of brick except for the four marble columns in the facade.

This use of brick — not as a mere economic expedient but as a valid element in the building even from the decorative point of view, so that it is left clearly visible — is typical of the architecture of this period. Buildings in Ostia and probably those in Rome were built with brick facades. Light reliefs, or polychrome effects obtained by the use of different materials, were the only decoration. From this point of view, funerary art is especially noteworthy: a change in rites, from cremation to interment, and the adoption of the marble sarcophagus (a custom from the Near East), created the need for more ample tomb spaces and led to the abandonment of the types of mausoleum used in the first century A.D. in favor of tombs in the form of a temple. Other forms analogous to these were used even in cases where the cremation rites persisted.

In the second century the tomb made entirely of brick prevails, with ample interior spaces — the type found, for example, in the necropolis at Isola Sacra (between Ostia and Portus), in the Vatican necropolis, or in the necropolis in Via Latina. A celebrated example is the tomb which has wrongly been called the mausoleum of Annia Regilla, the wife of Herodes Atticus. Here the use of brick has a high dignity, with refined effects of polychromy and carving.

THE CRISIS
The Imperial Age (A.D. 193-330)

The Socioeconomic Crisis of the Third Century

In A.D. 193 a new dynasty was brought into being when the legions of the Rhine and the Danube proclaimed Septimius Severus emperor, and forced the Senate to ratify their choice. The Severus family ruled until 235. With an able general at its head, the frontier problems of the Empire seemed capable of solution, at least temporarily; but the economic crisis of the Empire, though latent, merely grew worse during the course of those forty years, and exploded violently in the middle of the third century. Some projects planned by the Antonines were realized, such as the concession of Roman citizenship to all the inhabitants of the Empire. Caracalla made this move in A.D. 222, but for considerations that were basically economic: the Empire needed money.

After the death of Alexander Severus, the last of the dynasty, military anarchy reigned supreme in the Empire for more than fifty years. Emperors succeeded each other after periods of a few years, or sometimes even of a few months. Some provinces, such as Gaul and Palmyra (in Syria), gained de facto independence during this period. The collapse of the economy was most clearly seen in the devaluation of the official coin, the denarius, whose silver rate reached abysmal levels. The ranks of the state bureaucracy, which had functioned in the preceding century mainly with the consent of the provincial middle classes, now became almost purely confiscators of tribute, and the central authority was often respected only by means of brute force. Events that took place in other fields were linked to those in politics. The peculiar "national" character of the various cultures began to assert themselves within the population of the Empire, assuming an "anticlassical" character adverse to the Greco-Roman culture of the ruling class. Within that class itself, the disintegration of the economy and the society coincided with a collapse of all the ideological values on which Greco-Roman civilization had been founded, values whose heir and propagator the Empire was.

Historically considered, the profundity of the crisis seems to have been greatest in religion. During the third century, traditional beliefs were virtually eliminated in the Empire and the religions of salvation triumphed. Often of eastern origin, they penetrated in the lower classes. The upper class found comfort in evasive and vague philosophies such as Neoplatonism. The popular religious movements, among which Christianity was the most important, thus became a revolutionary force, which the state labored with every means at its disposal to repress — but in vain.

The confusion and breakup is seen in art as well. But here the Roman urban centers must be distinguished from the various provinces; even within the provinces themselves further distinctions must be made. Rome had a building boom during the Severian age, followed by an impressive collapse during the middle years of the century, with few new works realized, and many of these restorations. For example,

DECADENCE AND CRISIS IN THE THIRD CENTURY A.D. AS VIEWED BY A CONTEMPORARY

The winter does not afford the abundance of rain necessary for the nourishment of the seeds left in the earth; the summer does not offer such a torrid sunny climate as to permit the maturing of the ears of wheat; the spring does not bring enough fecundity of fruit. The exhausted and worn-out quarries yield ever smaller quantities of gold and silver; the springs seem to become more arid with every passing day.

There is less agriculture in the fields, less fishing in the sea, fewer troops in the encampments, less justice in the Forum, less loyalty in friendship, skill in the arts, discipline in customs.... The rays of the sun are paler and weaker at sunset, the moonlight has become feeble during the last nights; the tree that in its time was green and flourishing has grown deformed in the sterility of its old age, and the spring that was rich and abundant at the beginning sends forth only a few drops now that decrepitude weakens it. This is the sentence that lies heavy on the world; this is the law of God: that all that has grown, grows old, all that is strong becomes weak, and through a process of progressive infirmity and diminution, disappears.

ST. CYPRIAN: *Letter to Demetrian*

Rome: Arch of the Argentari. Dedicated to Septimius Severus by the merchants and bankers of the Forum Boarium in A.D. 204, as an inscription states, this Arch was probably the monumental entrance to the square. The decorative sculpture shows members of the Imperial family making sacrifices, and barbarian prisoners.

during the time of Gallienus (253–268), which represented a period of relative revival, the name of the emperor was celebrated simply by sculpturing an inscription on one of the gates of the ancient Servian wall rebuilt by Augustus. The most notable work of the period was dictated by necessity. This was the imposing urban boundary wall, which the emperor Aurelian had built in the years 271–275 to be the principal defense of the city against the barbarian hordes. (It was later enlarged by Honorius at the beginning of the fifth century.)

Most of the provinces also experienced some economic decline relative to their former prosperity; a negative gauge of the situation is the small number and small importance of the public works undertaken. There were some exceptions, however, in particular the African provinces, which seem to have been the richest part of the Empire in the third century. Their prosperity was due above all to agricultural and commercial factors — African oil, for example, replaced Spanish oil in the market — and it corresponded to an extraordinary cultural and artistic boom in Roman Africa, in literature, architecture, and the figurative arts. The mosaic art of these provinces, in particular, is one of the most remarkable products of ancient civilization.

Public Art of the Severian Age

The best example of official art in Rome during the time of Septimius Severus is the Arch of Septimius Severus, erected in the Roman Forum. The dedicatory inscription dates the arch at A.D. 203. It has three barrel vaults and very bold proportions. Only ten years passed between the Column of Marcus Aurelius and the Arch, and the stylistic character of the sculpture on the Arch, which celebrates the emperor's campaigns against the Parthians and the Arabs, does not differ much from that of the sculpture on the column. The four large panels that decorate the two facades are of particular interest. The scenes are arranged on many superimposed levels, which some scholars think indicates that they were planned for use in a column like Trajan's or Aurelius', but then adapted to an arch. It is more likely that the sculptures were taken from "sketches" like those in the triumphal paintings that had existed in Rome from the earliest periods of the Republic and whose most ancient specimen can be recognized in a

Rome: The Baths of Caracalla. Overall view. This building complex, the largest of its kind at the time (beginning of the third century A.D.) in Rome, lies at the end of the slopes of the little Avenine, near the Appian Way. The water for these baths was supplied by a branch of the Aqua Marcia, created especially for this purpose.

Rome: Plan of the Baths of Caracalla (first quarter of the third century A.D.).
1 Natatio (*pool*)
2 Great central hall
3 Tepidarium
4 Calidarium
5 Gymnasiums

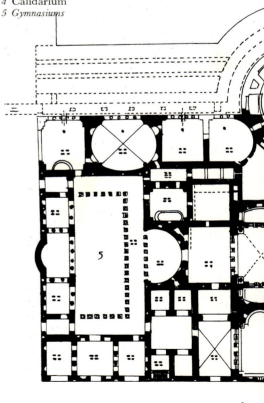

Let me die, if I think silence so absolutely necessary for a studious man as it seems at first to be: variety of noise surrounds me on every side: I lodge even over a public bath. Suppose now all kinds of sounds that can be harsh and disagreeable to the ears; as when strong boxers are exercising themselves, and sling about their hands loaded with lead, or when they are in distress, or imitate those that are, and I hear their groans; or when sending forth their breath, which for some time they held in, I hear their hissing and violent sobs; or when I meet with an idle varlet, who anoints the ordinary wrestlers with their exercise, and I hear the different slaps he gives them on their shoulder, with either a flat or hollow palm; or if a ballplayer comes in, and begins to count the balls, it is almost over with me. Add to these the rank and swaggering bully, the taking a pickpocket, or the bawling of such as delight to hear their voice echo through the bath; add also those who dash into the pool with a great noise of water; and besides these, such whose voices at least are tolerable: suppose a hair-plucker every now and then squeaking with a shrill and effeminate tone, to make himself the more remarkable, and is never silent but when he is at work, and making his patient cry for him; add to these the various cries of those that sell cakes and sausages, the gingerbread baker, the huckster, and all such as vend their wares about the streets with a peculiar tone.

SENECA: *Letter to Lucilius* (56)

Following pages:
The Alexandrian aqueduct in the Roman Campagna, the work of the last Emperor of the Severian dynasty, Alexander Severus.

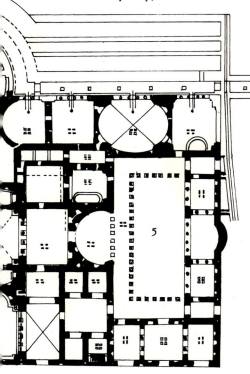

fresco from the Esquiline (illustrated on page 34). The ancient author Herodianus recalls that Septimius Severus sent some "commentaries" on his campaigns from the Near East, together with paintings that illustrated the details. Perhaps these were the originals for the sculpture found on the emperor's arch. If so, it is interesting that an emperor who came to power by force should desire to link himself to the obsolete traditions of the Republic, by the use of a report written to the Senate and by triumphal paintings.

Some of the iconographic and stylistic elements of these sculptures seem to hark back to "popular" motifs. This was characteristic of triumphal painting, and such motifs always reappear in the monuments of official art, even in those most closely connected to "cultured" artistic forms, such as the *Ara Pacis*, or in those rich in novelty, such as Trajan's Column. The disintegration of the organic classical form seems to have given new vitality to these motifs. In the four large sculptured panels and the frieze representative of triumph, qualities of plebeian art reappear. The bird's-eye views of cities are common to almost all historical depictions, but there are also indifference to perspective and to the characterization of landscape, schematic and repeated figures, a prevalence of the narrative and contextural aspects over the formal aspect of the work, to the point where the total composition is neglected altogether.

Formal novelties are noticeable only by examining some details, for the art of the third century is actually the antithesis of classical or Hellenistic art where the total vision prevails and all the elements are linked in an organic composition. Here, on the contrary, the vision is analytic. Every element has its own value per se. The art is "expressionistic" and "psychological," as seems suitable to an epoch in which the state bureaucracy and every other structure in the ancient world was disintegrating. Individuals were left to face the ideological vacuum as best they might, or retire into themselves in a spiritual attempt to recognize themselves as individuals. It is certainly no coincidence that the most valid genre of Roman art in this period is portraiture, which reaches a very high level of accomplishment.

At the same time, in some monuments of nonofficial art, such as the arch in the Forum Boarium dedicated to Septimius Severus in 204 by some bankers and merchants, the dissolution of plastic form reaches an even more advanced level. Its human figures are submerged in a thick net of non-figurative ornamental elements, which sculptors seem to have grown to prefer.

Development of the Imperial Baths: The Baths of Caracalla

Urban architecture in Rome realized some of its most amazing works during the Severian age. This persistence of building activity offers further evidence, should it be needed, of the way in which great urban architecture is an element unto itself, separate, to a certain extent, from the objective economic situation in the Empire, which finds a reflection in it only secondarily and always after a certain delay. The reason for this is clear. Since all this building activity had a symbolic function as part of the imperial apparatus, and was realized through a completely isolated organization in the hands of the emperor, it was relatively independent of the general economic conditions.

Among the most important achievements in this field were the enlargement of the Imperial palaces on the Palatine (by the construction of a luxurious monumental front), the Septizodium facing the Appian Way, the Severian Baths on the Palatine, the Temple of Serapis on the Quirinal, and above all the grandiose Baths of Caracalla. The latter is the most remarkable and best preserved example of

what are customarily called the "Great Imperial Baths." Architecturally there is a sharp difference between the older type of public baths — thermae — derived from the Greek gymnasium (the best examples are to be found in Pompeii and Herculaneum) and the new type of edifice that developed in Rome during the Imperial Age. In the older thermae the rooms were arranged in series, one after the other, and communicated directly with one another. This elementary system was possible as long as the size of the buildings and the number of "customers" remained limited. It thus continued to be used in the minor centers even when the new type of thermae had already been the fashion in the capital for some time.

This new form originated when the population in Rome became so large that it was necessary not only to increase the size and number of the public baths, but also to invent a more rational plan for them, able to absorb the masses of people in the most rapid and efficient way and at the same time capable of taking on a more monumental and "symbolic" aspect. Roman architecture had already faced such combinations of urban and monumental problems. The creation of the amphitheater, for instance, met needs not felt in ancient Greece. An increase in size of building types already known — the theater, the stadium, the gymnasium — would not have been sufficient to solve the problem, so new building types were created, perfectly suited to new functions and capable of handling large numbers of people. The history of building in Rome is well enough known so that the stages through which the Great Imperial Baths developed can be outlined.

The first installation of public baths on a large scale was built by Agrippa in the Campus Martius during the last part of the first century B.C., and was closely related to the urban reorganization planned by Augustus. Renaissance drawings show plans of this building. Although it was restored many times in the Imperial Age, it remained substantially like the type of "Minor Thermae" derived from the gymnasium.

The qualitative leap probably took place with Nero. The thermae begun by this emperor, also in the Campus Martius, are known both by their remains and through plans drawn by Renaissance artists. Although there is some dispute about the matter, it is unlikely that the restorations of Emperor Alexander Severus changed the basic plan of the building. In these baths the essential elements of the "Great Thermae" type are seen for the first time. The fundamental conception is the duplication of the smaller rooms, forming two perfectly symmetrical wings on the sides of an axis along which the fundamental services — the *calidarium* (hot room), the *tepidarium* (warm room), and *natatio* (large cold water pool) — are placed. At the center of the complex a large rectangular hall, a sort of large basilica usually identified wrongly with the *tepidarium*, communicates with the other rooms by means of two crossing axes. This arrangement allowed a large mass of people to follow the obligatory course of a traditional Roman bath — heat to provoke perspiration, ablutions with tepid water, and then the cold water pool — along two separate one-way courses, without going back through all the rooms. The actual bathing rooms, rather than being duplicated, were merely enlarged and used for both courses. Not only was this plan more rational and less expensive than a duplication of the fundamental rooms would have been, it allowed for monumental treatment. The rooms of the little baths, set one after the other, were replaced by an organic, coherent system with bilateral correspondences, focal nuclei and symmetrical axes.

THE AQUEDUCTS OF ROME

So that I may not accidentally omit anything necessary for understanding the whole subject, I shall first set down the names of the waters that are brought into the city of Rome; then by what persons and under which consuls and in what year since the founding of the city each was brought in; at what places and milestones their aqueducts commence; how far they are carried in underground channels, how far on masonry substructures, how far on arches; the height of each of them; the size and numbers of outlets and what uses are made of them; how much water each aqueduct brings to each section outside the city and how much within the city; how many public delivery tanks there are and how much they deliver to places of public amusement, to ornamental fountains — as the educated call them — and to water basins; how much water is assigned to the use of the State (in Caesar's name) and how much to private uses by grant of the emperor; what is the law concerning construction and maintenance of the aqueducts; and what penalties enforce the law under various regulations, votes of the Senate, and Imperial edicts. . . . For 441 years since the foundation of the city, Romans were satisfied to use the waters they drew from the Tiber, from wells, or from springs. Down to the present day, springs have been given the name of holy things and are objects of veneration; they have the repute of healing the sick, as for example the spring of the Prophetic Nymphs of Apollo and the spring of Juturna. . . Under the consulate of M. Valerius Maximus and P. Decius Mus, in the thirtieth year (313 B.C.) after the outset of the war with the Samnians, the Appian water was brought into the city by the censor Appius Claudius Crassus. He also was responsible for constructing the Appian Way, from Porta Capena to the city of Capua. . . .

FRONTINUS:
The Water Supply of Rome (4)

This arrangement appears at a single blow in the age of Nero and may be the work of a single person. An age of architectural novelty and of important artists — such as the architects of the *Domus Aurea*, Severus and Celer — Nero's reign also saw important urban innovations. After the terrible fire of A.D. 64, a new city, the *nova urbs* mentioned by ancient authors, seems to have been conceived according to more rational and modern criteria than had been previously applied. More than an architectural phenomenon, the great baths are a town-planning phenomenon of the first order. Even if the plan of the baths of Nero is not the original plan, but one of the Severian age, the invention of the type need be moved only a few years, for it occurred again in the Thermae of Titus, in about A.D. 80. The next built were the Thermae of Trajan, which rose on the Oppian Hill near the Colosseum on the remains of the *Domus Aurea* between A.D. 104 and 109. By this time the great thermae type is definite and mature; it was not later modified significantly. Nor are the Baths of Trajan inferior in scale to the two grandiose complexes that followed it in Rome, the Baths of Caracalla (212–216) and the Baths of Diocletian (298–306). These three complexes, separated by nearly a century from each other, seem to mark emblematically the fundamental stages of Roman urban architecture. The architect of the Baths of Trajan was the great Apollodorus of Damascus, creator also of the Forum of Trajan.

Of the three great complexes the Baths of Caracalla is in the best state of preservation. Like the other two, it included a great perimetrical wall with an exedra — or perhaps the tiers of a theater — measuring approximately 1105 by 1076 feet. At the center of this enclosure — first seen in the Baths of Trajan — stood the thermal building proper, which measured some 722 by 374 feet, and was built to the plan described above. Space between the wall and the building was used for gardens, and the rooms set into the outside perimeter included two libraries. The Baths of Caracalla is remarkable not only in its size, but in its structural achievements as well. The greater circular calidarium was covered with a cupola over 111 feet in diameter, not much smaller than that of the Pantheon, but more advanced in its technique of construction; the large windows placed in the walls beneath the dome required the solution of quite complex problems in statics. The central hall is covered with three grandiose cross-vaults. Only the bare skeleton of the complex remains today, but enough of the original marble, mosaic, and sculptural decoration has remained to show that the functions of the bath were not exclusively utilitarian. Its artistic level was equal to that of the Imperial palaces, as were its costs. The best artists and architects of the time were employed; huge pieces of sculpture (now in the National Museum in Naples) exemplify the high accomplishment of the decorative work.

The baths were frequented by the Roman plebeians, the people of the lower class for whom the free distribution of food and the games of the circus and the amphitheater had alike been organized by the state. The term "villas of the poor," which was applied to the great thermal complexes of Imperial Rome, is on the whole correct. They were public works, but they were also works of propaganda, exaltations of imperial munificence. The living quarters of ancient Rome were a great contrast to these buildings of extraordinary luxury, dark and dank multistoried buildings where many families were crowded together in limited and unhealthy space fit only for the nightly rest. Normal life was led outside these slums; in the forums in good weather, in winter in the thermae that were numerous and spacious enough to take in thousands of people every day. Besides the advantage of the baths, they offered numerous other attractions: heating, which was nonexistent in private dwelling; libraries; gardens and spectacles of various kinds. A brief reflection on the function of buildings like the Baths of Caracalla reveals a great deal about the social and political structure of the Empire. The immense plebeian masses of the cities were bound to the emperor in a thoroughly paternalistic relationship.

Construction at Ostia

Ostia, the port of Rome (two-thirds of which has been brought to light by excavations), gives an indirect but rather faithful picture of the nonofficial building that took place in Rome between the second and third centuries. The period of Ostia's greatest building activity was during Hadrian's reign, when new construction covered about 160,000 square yards. In the period between Antoninus Pius and Commodus the land used for new works decreased to about 66,000 square yards. And the decrease was accentuated from the Severian emperors on. In all the third century, not more than 45,000 square yards of buildings were erected in Ostia. The decrease is even more impressive if it is borne in mind that most of the activity in the last period was not new construction, but rather restoration. There was also a sharp curve downward during the course of the third century. In the Severian period important public works were undertaken, such as the Baths of Porta Marina and the Round Temple, but they were completely lacking in the second half of the century. The picture of general stagnation which Ostia shows corresponds perfectly to the situation in the nearby capital.

The theater at Ostia, built in the Augustan Age, was restored at the end of the second century, with an increase of three or four thousand in its seating capacity. Although the dedication took place under Septimius Severus and Caracalla in A.D. 196, the work was done almost entirely during the reign of Commodus. At the end of the second century the enormous increase in population led to an attempt to enlarge the capacity of public buildings. At the same time the great Piazza of the Corporations, behind the theater, was restored; this was a large porticoed area with a series of cells that were the offices of representatives of the navigation and trading companies of the principal Mediterranean cities. The inscriptions on the mosaics set in front of these cells indicate in fact the "nationality" of the *navicularii* (shipowners) and the *negotiatores* (merchants) who had their offices here. An entire side of the portico was occupied by representatives from African cities, further proof of the economic importance of these provinces during this period. No other ancient monument gives a more lively and direct picture of the varied and complex economic structure of the Roman Empire.

The Aurelian Walls

The most important construction in Rome in the second half of the third century was military, and, moreover, defensive: the Aurelian walls. After the initial period of the Republic, the city had no boundary wall. The Roman conquests, which had expanded the confines of the ancient city-state to include the entire Mediterranean area, rendered such a work superfluous. The real defensive line was the *limes*, that gigantic fortification work that almost everywhere follows the borders of the Empire. The first symptom of danger to Rome itself during the Imperial period took place during the reign of Marcus Aurelius, when the northeastern frontiers of Italy were violated for the first time in centuries, and the Quadi and Marcomanni pushed down to Aquileia (west of present–day Trieste). The invasions of the Alamanni, which multiply from A.D. 258 on, showed how easy it was to penetrate deeply into Italy. The capital itself came to seem a frontier post that needed a solid wall for its protection.

The person who saw to its construction was Aurelian (A.D. 270–275), who had to do without the help of the military workers who were specialists in jobs of this kind; they were then engaged in the war against Palmyra. The work was thus entrusted to building corporations in the city. It proceeded at a remarkably rapid pace. The walls were finished in four years, a sure sign that danger was considered imminent.

Rome: The Catacombs of Priscilla on the Via Salaria. The so-called Greek chapel. Third Century A.D.

POPE DAMASO'S INSCRIPTION IN THE CATACOMBS OF ST. SEBASTIAN

O you, whoever you be, who search for the names of Peter and Paul, you must know that at one time the bodies of these saints lay here. The Orient sent them here as disciples (of Christ), we admit this most heartily. Through the blood they shed, following Christ amidst the stars they reached the gates of heaven and the kingdom of the just. Rome deserved more than the other cities to claim them as her citizens. Damaso here sings your praises, O you new stars.

AURELIAN BUILDS THE WALLS OF ROME

When the war with the Marcomanni was ended, Aurelian, over-violent by nature, and now filled with rage, advanced to Rome eager for the revenge which the bitterness of the revolts had prompted. . . . Then, since all that happened made it seem possible that some such thing might occur again, as had happened under Gallienus, after asking advice from the senate, he extended the walls of the city of Rome. The pomerium, however, he did not extend at that time, but later.

Scriptores Historiae Augustae (XXI)

INSCRIPTION ON THE PORTA MAGGIORE

The Senate and People of Rome set this up to the Imperial Caesars, our Lords the two princes Arcadius and Honorius, victorious, triumphant, ever Augusti, to commemorate the restoration of the walls, gates, and towers of the Eternal City, after the removal of huge quantities of rubble. At the suggestion of the distinguished and noble Count Stilicho, Master of both of the Armed Forces, their statues were set up to preserve the memory of their name. Flavius Macrobius Longinianus, City Prefect, devoted to their majesty and divine power, was in charge of the work.

Corpus Inscriptionum Latinarum (VI:1189)

The haste with which the work was done is seen in, among other things, the relative unpretentiousness of the work — the wall was barely twenty feet high and eleven feet thick — and also in the fact that many preexisting constructions were included in it or swallowed up by it — the pyramid of Cestius, the facades of houses, tombs, and at times aqueducts, as at Porta Maggiore. Even with its limited dimensions, the work must have appeared sufficient to contain any attack by the barbarian hordes. For the most part they did not have the implements necessary for a siege, and although the initial ferocity of their attacks was great, they could not stage a long siege because of their poor logistical situation. In their present state, the Aurelian Walls are the result of much restoration and reconstruction work, the most important of which took place under Honorius at the beginning of the fifth century. On that occasion the height of the walls and of the square towers that rise up every hundred feet was doubled, numerous minor gates that weakened the fortification were sealed off, and the openings of other gates were narrowed.

Today these walls, for the most part preserved over their total length of almost twelve miles, are the most imposing fortification remaining from the ancient world. Thoroughly functional, they were in uninterrupted use up to the last century. Of the infinite number of medieval,

Rome: The Aurelian Walls. Porta San Sebastiano (once Porta Appia). A reconstruction built during the reign of Honorius, at the beginning of the fifth century A.D., of the city gate of the third century.

Following pages:
A stretch of the Aurelian Walls. Built by the Emperor Aurelian between A.D. 270 and 275, and enlarged and reinforced by Arcadius and Honorius in 403, this well-preserved and imposing wall is about twelve miles long. The square towers appear every 100 feet.

Renaissance and modern restorations, the most notable is the grandiose bastion built by Sangallo during the Renaissance. The short battle at the wall that ended with the capture of Rome in 1870 by the forces of United Italy and the ill-fated uprising against Nazi occupation after September 8, 1943 at Porta San Paulo are further confirmation of the part these walls have played in Roman history.

Besides the historical continuity that has made the Aurelian Walls perhaps the most significant monument in the city, they offer a documentary history of the extension of ancient Rome. The area inside the wall boundary is about 3,410 acres. Not all of this enormous space was covered by construction; the course of the walls was also chosen on the basis of strategic criteria. But it is still a most valuable indication of the size the city had reached. Then, too, some points of the wall take on an immense documentary value, when seen in the perspective of history. A typical case is Porta San Sebastiano, the ancient Porta Appia, the most imposing of all. It opens onto the ancient consular way of 312 B.C., attributed to the censor Appius, the first and most important opening for Roman expansionism and imperialism, going south and east. Here within only a few miles, some of the city's most significant monuments were built, from the sepulcher of the Scipios, among the first and most consistent supporters of Roman imperialism,

tury, when a great many factories were hard at work at the same time turning out products for the great enterprises of official construction. As noted earlier, after the Severian period, building activity in Rome fell off sharply. The material used in the Aurelian walls belonged largely to older buildings demolished at the time the walls were being erected. Thus, for construction of the Baths of Diocletian a building industry had to be renewed from the bottom up. It was entirely under the control of the emperor, who owned all the brick factories. The revival was of brief duration, however. The industry entered a new decadence after the capital was transferred to Constantinople in A.D. 330.

The fire that devastated Rome in A.D. 283 should be mentioned in relation to the building activity under Diocletian. The Curia Julia in the Forum and the Pompeian Porticoes in the Campus Martius were restored following this disaster, taking the epithets "Jovian" and "Herculean" respectively, from the epithets of the two emperors.

The Arch of Galerius, the most important monument of official sculpture in the period, lies outside Rome, at Salonica in Greece. In Rome, however, one of the foundations built on the rostra of the Roman Forum on the occasion of the tenth anniversary of the government of Diocletian — *decennalia* — still exists. Here two sides, one depicting the victories of the emperor and the other his sacrifices, were executed

Rome: The Basilica of Maxentius (or of Constantine), begun by Maxentius between A.D. 306 and 310 and finished by Constantine. The main entrance was originally on the eastern side (upper right), with an apse at the western end. Constantine built another entrance to the south, toward the Via Sacra. In the apse there was a colossal statue of the Emperor (now in the courtyard of the Palazzo dei Conservatori). The northern side of this structure has remained practically intact, whereas almost nothing remains of the southern side and the gigantic central cross-vault.

Spalato (Split): Plan of the Palace of Diocletian
1 *Porta Aurea*
2 *Porta Argentea*
3 *Porta Bronzea*
4 *Porta Ferrea*
5 *Court and Temple of Jupiter*
6 *Court and Mausoleum of Diocletian*
7 *Vestibule*
8 *The so-called Tablinum*

Rome: Detail of the Basilica of Maxentius.

ELEGY OF THE TETRARCHY

O spring, so happy and blessed because of this new fruit, not so glad and venerable now because of the beauty of the flowers or the green growth of your messengers or the buds of your vines, and not even because of your breezes and serene light, but rather because of the apparition of the supreme Caesars! . . . How many centuries in fact, O invincible princes, do you secure for yourselves and for the state, dividing among yourselves the dominion of the world that belongs to you? As safe as it is now, since all the enemies have been subdued, this dominion nonetheless requires too many repeated journeys to places very distant from one another. Now, Parthia cast beyond the Tigris, Dacia regained, the borders of Germany and Rhaetia brought to the sources of the Danube, the punishment of Brittany and Batavia assured, the state — enlarged and to be enlarged — still required a broader government, and those who had extended the boundaries of Roman power with their worth were duty-bound to render a son who would share in this power.

Moreover, not to speak of the interest and care of the state, even that majesty that related them to Jove and Hercules required for the Jovian and Herculean emperors something similar to what exists in the universe and in the very heavens. And in fact all the greatest things shine and rejoice in this characteristic number of your divinity: there are four elements, and as many seasons, and four parts of the world divided by two oceans and the lustra that return after a quadruple revolution of the sky, and there are four horses of the sun, and Vesperus and Lucifer who are added to the two principal lights in the heavens.

Panegyric of Constantinius Chlorus

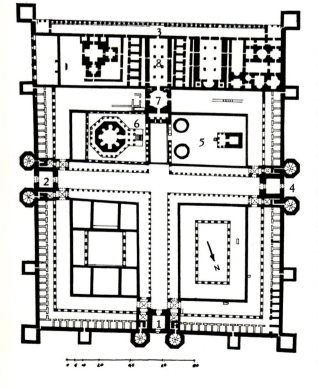

in the style typical of the third century, with extensive use of the drill to carve the surface of the marble. The drill cuts out and isolates each detail sharply from the rest. The other two sides, depicting the sacrifice of the pig, the sheep, and the bull — *suovetaurilia* — and the procession of the senators, are executed with a pure and simple drawing technique, and are more plastic in feeling. On these, the drill was used only moderately. One of the most typical formal characteristics of the high Tetrarchic period is precisely this return to a highly compact and bounded plastic vision, with few details, lightly incised. This is to be seen especially in the portraits, in which the expressionism at times goes so far that the images border on the frankly brutal. Particularly suitable to this style are the hard Egyptian stones such as porphyry. It was used, among other things, for the celebrated "Tetrarchs" in the Basilica of St. Mark in Venice. The origin of those sculptures in Constantinople was demonstrated only recently, following the discovery there of a foot belonging to one of the personages in the group.

The closed, rigidly hierarchical, centralized and militaristic vision typical of Diocletian characterized the entire period and is clearly to be seen in the best preserved of the Imperial residences, that at Spalato (Split in present–day Yugoslavia), which the emperor built as a retreat where he could spend the rest of his life after his abdication.

It is highly instructive to compare this closed, geometrical structure, closer to a medieval castle than to an Imperial residence, and the loose, open, and varied plan of Hadrian's Villa. They not only express two totally different personalities; they reflect the differences between two eras.

The Projects of Maxentius

Building activity at Rome continued at a particularly high rate under Maxentius, who chose the city as his capital. In the course of his short reign (306–312), this unfortunate emperor managed to plan and in part complete an outstanding series of buildings, most of which have been preserved in fairly good condition. A considerable part of this activity was centered in the Forum. Among the edifices built here were the grandiose basilica, completed by Constantine, and in its immediate vicinity, the small temple that has erroneously been called the sanctuary of Romulus, the emperor's son, who died in boyhood and was at once deified. The basilica in particular, with its vast, imposing vaults, similar to those built a few years earlier by the architects of the Baths of Diocletian, presents an outstanding example of the technical capabilities of the Roman workmen. Brought to completion in this period, in addition to the basilica, was the reconstruction of the Temple of Venus and Rome, originally erected during the reign of Hadrian. In all probability it was only at this later time that the coffered vaults and the two opposite apses, destined to contain the statues of the two divinities, were built.

It is interesting that it was Maxentius who reconstructed the work of Hadrian, for, like Hadrian, Maxentius also desired to live in an elaborate suburban villa and began to build one, superimposed above part of the *Pago Triopio* of Herodes Atticus, on the Appian Way. The complex is made up of three large building groups: the villa itself, the great mausoleum of Romulus with its surrounding quadri–portico, and the circus, each oriented in a different direction but all converging on one center. The mausoleum is a good example of a type fairly widespread in the fourth century. It is circular in shape and has two levels. The lower was composed of a ring-like corridor around a central pillar with niches for sarcophagi; the upper was built for the worship of the deified deceased, and was covered with a cupola. The circus should be considered in close connection with the mausoleum, because here it again assumed its original function, a place for the celebration of funereal games.

By chance this latter monument has been preserved in good condition. Its documentary value is extremely important since virtually nothing remains of the other circuses, including the most imposing, the Circus Maximus. The eight *carceres*, the stalls from which the quadrigas (the four-horse chariots) departed are recognizable in the Circus of Maxentius. The numbers of the quadrigas correspond with those of the four *factiones* — teams — that divided the allegiance of the spectators. Each team had a right to two quadrigas. The carceres were laid out radically and on a slightly inclined surface, to equalize the course of the quadrigas during the first part of the race. The right side of the track, traversed first, is wider than the other, to allow for the passing of several chariots side by side before the first eliminations. For the same reason, the straight stretch of the circus began at a considerable distance (some 650 feet) from the point of departure. All told, the contestants had to circle the course seven times; the overall distance of the race was about two and one-half miles.

Many ancient sculptures were used in decorating the circus. They were no doubt taken from monuments that had been demolished or stripped; among other things found here was the obelisk, still later used by Bernini for the fountain in Piazza Navona. The inscription

Outskirts of Rome: The Circus of Maxentius. Side with starting point stall for the chariots and two towers. Built by Maxentius as part of his villa and the mausoleum of his son Romulus, along the Appian Way, in the location formerly occupied by the villa of Herodes Atticus, the circus was never finished. Work was interrupted by the death of the Emperor after his defeat at the Milvian bridge.

THE COLOSSEUM AS DESCRIBED IN A MEDIEVAL GUIDE TO ROME

The Colosseum was the Temple of the Sun, of marvelous greatness and beauty, disposed with many diverse vaulted chambers and all covered with a heaven of gilded brass, where thunders and lightnings and glittering fires were made, and where rain was shed through slender tubes. Besides this there were the signs supercelestial and the planets, Sol and Lune, that were drawn along in their chariots. And in the midst abode Phoebus, that is the god of the Sun, which having his feet on the earth reached unto heaven with his head, and did hold in his hand an orb, signifying that Rome ruled over the world.

But after a space of time, the blessed Silvester bade destroy the temple, and in like wise other palaces, to the intent that the orators which came to Rome should not wander through profane buildings, but shall pass with devotion through the churches. But the head and hands of the aforesaid idol he caused to be laid before his Palace of the Lateran in remembrance thereof; and the same is now called by the vulgar, Samson's Ball. And before the Colosseum was a temple, where ceremonies were done to the aforesaid image.

The Marvels of Rome

THE VISIT OF CONSTANTINE II TO ROME (A.D. 357)

So then he entered Rome, the home of empire and of every virtue, and when he had come to the Rostra, the most renowned forum of ancient dominion, he stood amazed; and on every side on which his eyes rested he was dazzled by the array of marvellous sights. He addressed the nobles in the senate-house and the populace from the tribunal, and being welcomed to the palace with manifold attentions, he enjoyed a longed-for pleasure; and on several occasions, when holding equestrian games, he took delight in the sallies of the commons, who were neither presumptuous nor regardless of their old-time freedom, while he himself also respectfully observed the due mean. For he did not (as in the case of other cities) permit the contests to be terminated at his own discretion, but left them (as the custom is) to various chances. Then, as he surveyed the sections of the city and its suburbs, lying within the summits of the seven hills, along their slopes, or on level ground, he thought that whatever first met his gaze towered above all the rest: the sanctuaries of Tarpeian Jove so far surpassing as things divine excel those of earth; the baths built up to the measure of provinces; the huge bulk of the amphitheater, strengthened by its framework of Tiburtine stone, to whose top human eyesight barely ascends; the Pantheon like a rounded city-district, vaulted over in lofty beauty; and the exalted heights which rise with platforms to which one may mount, and bear the likenesses of former emperors; the Temple of the City, the Forum of Peace, the Theater of Pompey, the Oleum, the Stadium, and amongst these the other adornments of the Eternal City.

But when he came to the Forum of Trajan, a construction unique under the heavens, as we believe, and admirable even in the unanimous opinion of the gods, he stood fast in amazement, turning his attention to the gigantic complex about him, beggaring description and never again to be imitated by mortal men. Therefore abandoning all hope of attempting anything like it, he said that he would and could copy Trajan's steed alone, which stands in the centre of the vestibule, carrying the emperor himself. To this, prince Ormisda, who was standing near him, and whose departure from Persia I have described above, replied with native wit: "First, Sire," said he, "command a like stable to be built, if you can; let the steed which you propose to create range as widely as this which we see." When Ormisda was asked directly what he thought of Rome, he said that he took comfort in this fact alone, that he had learned that even there men were mortal. So then, when the emperor had viewed many objects with awe and amazement, he complained of Fame as either incapable or spiteful, because while always exaggerating everything, in describing what there is in Rome, she becomes shabby. And after long deliberation what he should do there, he determined to add to the adornments of the city by erecting in the Circus Maximus an obelisk, the provenance and figure of which I shall describe in the proper place.

AMMIANUS MARCELLINUS:
History (13-17)

Rome: The so-called temple of Romulus on the Via Sacra. This small octagonal structure, built at the beginning of the fourth century A.D., still has its original bronze door. Today it is part of the church of SS. Cosma and Damiano.

on it, in hieroglyphics, bears the name of Domitian; it was almost certainly taken from the temple of Isis and Serapis in the Campus Martius, near the Pantheon, built during Domitian's reign. The trip made by the obelisk in different periods for different purposes is certainly a curious one. It was altogether normal, of course, for such a monument to belong to a temple devoted to Egyptian divinities: other smaller obelisks found at the Villa of Maxentius, in fact, came from the Temple of Isis in the Campus Martius. It has often been noted that this custom of reusing elements taken from buildings of various periods bears witness to a decadence in Rome's artistic workshops, and an inability to carry out extensive new undertakings.

It also suggests a pronounced eclectic taste in Rome, typical of a city of once-great artistic traditions that finds itself constantly on the sidelines. It had lost its true function as the administrative and political capital of the Empire. This withdrawal into nostalgia and conservation of the past is typical of a culture that is losing its vitality. The sense of an inevitable decadence leads to an attempt to recover the past at all costs, to save and pass on to posterity all that is best from a civilization. Encyclopedias, commentaries, and anthologies were assembled beginning at this time, and are a gold mine of information on almost every aspect of ancient culture. It is partly this nostalgia that must have inspired them. The rebirth of paganism at the end of the fourth century, when the Christian empire had long been an established fact, can be considered in the same light.

Rome: The Temple of Venus and Roma. The cella facing the Forum, seen here, is the better preserved of the two; statues of the two gods were placed in them. The rich decoration of the floor and walls, with the porphyry columns, as well as the coffered vault, can be dated in the reign of Maxentius, during which the building, originally erected in the age of Hadrian, was restored following a fire (A.D. 307).

INSCRIPTION ON THE
ARCH OF CONSTANTINE

To the Emperor Caesar Flavius Constantinus Maximus, Pius, Felix, Augustus — since through the inspiration of the Deity, and in the greatness of his own mind, he with his army avenged the Commonwealth with arms rightly taken up, and at a single time defeated the Tyrant and all his Faction — the Senate and People of Rome dedicated this Arch adorned with Triumphs.

Rome: The four-faced arch of the Forum Boarium. Constantinian Age.

INVENTORY OF ROME
IN FOURTH CENTURY (A.D.)

2	Temples of Jupiter Capitolinus
2	Circuses
2	Amphitheaters
2	Colossi
2	Spiral Columns
2	Markets
3	Theaters
4	Gladiators' Barracks
2	Naumachias (for water spectacles)
15	Nymphaeums
22	Large equestrian statues
80	Golden statues of gods
74	Ivory statues of gods
36	Marble arches
37	City-wall gates
423	Streets
423	Shrines
46,602	Ordinary homes
1,790	Luxury houses
260	Storehouses
856	Public baths
1,352	Basins
254	Ovens
46	Brothels
144	Public toilets
10	Praetorian stations (imperial guards)
4	Urban police stations
7	Fire stations
14	First aid stations
2,300	Centers for olive oil distribution

Regional Catalogues (Age of Constantine)

Rome: The Arch of Constantine. Erected after the battle against Maxentius in A.D. 312 and dedicated in 315-316, the Arch is the largest and best preserved of the three remaining in Rome. The sculpture dates to various periods. On the sides of the attic, or top section, with the inscription, there are four reliefs from the age of Commodus depicting scenes from the life of Marcus Aurelius. The four statues of Dacians belong to the age of Trajan, as do the reliefs (not visible here) on the short sides of the attic and inside the central barrel vault. The four tondi (round relief panels) with scenes of hunting and sacrifice belong to a monument from Hadrian's time, as do the four on the other side. The reliefs above the two side vaults are Constantinian, as are the figures on the spandrels of the arches and the pedestals of the columns.

The Arch of Constantine and the Decline of Pagan Culture

The most typical and best-known example of this eclectic use of materials of various origins was the Arch of Constantine. But before moving on to an examination of its formal aspect, it would be well to place this monument, one of the most significant in ancient Rome, in its historical framework. The Arch was built by the Senate after Constantine's victory over Maxentius at the Milvian Bridge in A.D. 312, in memory of this triumph; it was not officially dedicated until the year 315. As early as 313, however, Constantine and Licinius, the emperor of the west appointed by Galerius, meeting in Milan, had granted Christians freedom of worship. The Arch's inscription speaks of a victory owed to "divine inspiration" and has helped strengthen the legend of a Constantine who was a Christian even at the time of the battle of the Milvian Bridge. The insertion of sculptures of clearly pagan significance, such as the two tondi (round panels) with the sun and the moon, should be enough to demonstrate this was not the case, however. Constantine's interest in the Christians was primarily political in nature rather than religious. By granting them freedom of worship, the emperor managed to win over to the side of the state the followers of a religion that was by now by far the most important in the Empire.

The sculptures of the Constantinian age that adorn the arch, representing the various episodes of the war against Maxentius, clearly belong to the "popular" vein, the same sort was frequently in minor friezes and in other triumphal arches, such as the Arch of Titus and that of Septimius Severus. Simplification, narrative clarity, a perspective by now altogether conventional, a hierarchical arrangement of personages, and frontality are all used. These characteristics have already been noted in more ancient sculptures, but here they reach a new level of systematic and stylistic coherence. The sculptures on the Arch of Constantine mark the completion of the total formal revolution that had begun with Tetrarchic art. They have a good deal more in common with the Romanesque achievements of the twelfth century than with the culture, chronologically much closer, of the Middle Empire.

The Arch of Constantine was one of the last official works in Rome. With the founding of the new capital, Constantinople, in A.D. 330, the old capital was once again abandoned, and Imperial building activity was replaced with new religious building, which took hold with extraordinary vigor. In a few decades it transformed the city altogether. The form of the pagan basilica was adopted for the new type of Christian edifice: a great hall with three or four naves separated by columns, ending in an apse. Continuing side by side with this type was the circular building covered by a cupola, adopted especially for mausoleums; some examples are those of the Gordiani in Via Praenestina, of Sant'Elena on the Via Labicana, and of Constantina (now Santa Costanza) on the Via Nomentana, a fine example of a cupola resting on a double colonnade, surrounded by a vaulted ambulatory. There was an extraordinary expansion in these years of the art of the wall mosaic. Examples from the initial and middle Imperial periods are relatively modest, but from this period on they were fundamental to artistic culture. Santa Costanza itself furnishes one of the finest examples.

Along with the exceptional efflorescence of Christian religious architecture, a pagan culture lived on for a long while in Rome, where it was nourished by the great aristocratic families, among them the Simmaci. Altogether "intellectual," it was a reactionary manifestation, produced by a class rapidly heading toward decadence, although it remained politically important until the end of the century. The program of tenacious conservation had a certain historical validity.

But how did that slave who for so many years had worn the imperial purple (Maxentius) arrange the army? In such a way that no one could flee in any manner, or as usually occurs, retreat and then resume fighting: in fact, it was closed in between your army and the Tiber . . . .

What other hope must it be thought nourished that one, who already for two days had abandoned the palace and with his wife and son had withdrawn voluntarily to a private dwelling, tormented by terrible dreams and hounded by nocturnal furies, so that you, the longed-for tenant, could succeed him in those sacred palaces after long expiatory purification ceremonies? At that point he himself had realized the reality of the situation and moved aside to let you pass him: although he set forth, armed, to do battle, from the time he had left the palace he had already abdicated. At the first sight of your majesty, and with the first surge of your many-times victorious army, the enemies were terrorized and fled; their retreat was blocked by the narrowness of the Milvius Bridge.

Thus, if we exclude those principally responsible for that government of bandits, who, despairing of any pardon, covered with their corpses the place they had chosen for the battle, all the others threw themselves headlong into the river, as if they wanted to offer a little respite to the arms of your men who were tired out from the massacre. The Tiber quickly swallowed up those impious ones; and even their leader, with his horse and splendid weapons, despite his vain attempts to save himself by going up the steep slope of the far bank, was dragged away by a whirlpool and disappeared. Thus it was impossible for that monster to leave behind even this bit of fame and glory: to wit, that he had died under the blows of a valorous soldier's sword or spear. The swirling river dragged away the bodies and weapons of the other enemies, but kept its own enemy in the same place in which it had died, so that the Roman people would have no doubts: someone might have thought that he had saved himself if the proof of his death had been lacking.

Holy Tiber, you who were once the counselor of your guest Aeneas, and later the savior of Romulus, who had been abandoned in your current, you could not bear the idea that a false Roman should live any longer and that the assassin of the city should save himself by swimming in your waters: you . . . rightly wanted to take part in Constantine's victory: he has thrown your enemy into your current, and you have killed him. . . . When the body was found and mutilated, all the Roman people abandoned themselves to the joy of revenge. His sacrilegious head was taken all round the city, impaled on a pole, and no one missed the opportunity to abuse it.

. . . The very houses, so I have been told, seemed to move, and their height seemed to increase, wherever your divinity was transported by the chariot that went forward slowly, so great was the crowd and so dense the Senate, that pushed you forward and at the same time held you back. Those who were farthest away called those who could see you better, fortunate. Those you had already passed before seemed to mourn for the place they had had. From every direction everyone in turn hastened to follow you. The enormous crowd thronged and swept in various directions: one was struck by the fact that so many had survived after the massacres of those six years of utter madness. Some dared to ask you to stop, and complained that you had reached the palace so quickly. Once you were inside, they not only followed you with their eyes, but almost rushed inside the sacred threshold. Then, being scattered in all the streets, they began to wait, to look for, desire, hope for, your exit. It almost seemed they were besieging him who had liberated them from a veritable siege.

Panegyric of Constantine

Rome: Wall painting from the residence of
the heralds at the foot of the Palatine. Third
century A.D.

Scholars associated with such groups produced the collections of information noted earlier; among them were Servius, the commentator on Virgil, and Macrobius, the writer and philosopher. Members of the pagan party also carried out work in architecture and the figurative arts. As late as A.D. 393 or 394 the prefect of provisions, Numerius Proiectus, restored the Temple of Hercules at Ostia, although in 391 Theodosius had ordered the closing of all pagan temples.

It was perhaps in these years that the masterpieces of Greek sculpture then in Rome were given inscriptions bearing the names of their creators. Acutely aware of the crisis at hand, as well as of the collapse of ancient culture, these groups made an attempt to save as much as possible from the impending darkness. For that matter the cultured Christian class itself, from St. Jerome to Cassiodorus, shared this mood and took part in the salvaging operation. Their combined efforts paved the way, through the Middle Ages, for the rediscovery of ancient culture — in the last analysis, for the Renaissance.

Nevertheless, the difference between pagan and Christian was fundamental. The pagans were purely "conservative." The Christians had the tendency to save and integrate into the new situation only elements of ancient culture that were compatible with Christian doctrine. Their disagreement exploded violently in the argument concerning the statue of Victory, which had been in the Senate since the time of Augustus. Simmacus and Saint Ambrose were the protagonists in the polemical battle that raged over this statue. The letters of these two personalities to the Emperor Valentinian II, which have been preserved, are among the most important documents for any understanding of this particular historical juncture.

Ambrose won in the end and the pagan statue was removed. It could not have ended otherwise. While buildings dedicated to the Christian religion were going up everywhere, the ancient city was falling bit by bit into decay. The emperors attempted in vain to put a stop to the sacking of the remaining monuments (the texts of various edicts to this effect exist) or to intervene by ordering restoration work done. While Rome was still intact in all its splendor at the time of the visit of Constantius II, the son of Constantine, who was greatly impressed, in the fifth century one disaster followed another. The strengthening of the walls by Honorius did not prevent the Goths of Alaric from capturing the city and sacking it. The damage that resulted was probably not too great; the sack of the city by the Vandals in 455 was much more serious. But the sensation created by the sack of the Goths was tremendous; echoes of it can be found in many of the writings of the period.

With the advent of the Emperor Theodoric there was a resumption of the work of preservation. Several monuments were restored, the Colosseum among them. But the war with the Goths, with all its sieges, sackings, massacres, was the city's coup de grace; among other things the aqueducts were all but completely destroyed. After the Gothic war, there was little to be seen in the enormous, deserted area inside the Aurelian walls except a few scattered hovels and lean-tos among the ruins. The decline of population, the desolation and insecurity of the surrounding countryside, infested with malaria and brigands, became irreversible, and were to characterize the city for centuries. It is only relatively recently that the last vestiges of these conditions have disappeared from Rome so that the heritage of its civilization and the greatness of its monuments have once more become apparent to all.

Rome: The so-called Temple of Minerva Medica. Beginning of the fourth century A.D. It is perhaps a Nympheum from the villa of the Licinii, built to a ten-sided plan, with niches. The circular cupola, one of the largest in Rome, over eighty feet in diameter, is set on brick ribbing. The building technique, much more advanced than that of the Pantheon, goes a long way toward that used by the Byzantines.

Right:
Mausoleum of the villa of the Gordiani, on the Via Praenestina. A typical monumental sepulcher of the fourth century A.D., similar to the mausoleum of the Romulus. There is a lower room, which is the burial chamber proper, and an upper hall used for the celebration of funeral rites.

Page 172:
Rome: Santa Costanza. Detail from the vault of the church's ambulatory, once the mausoleum of Constantina. Fourth century A.D. The use of wall mosaics, begun at the end of the Republican Age, spread until they became the leading art form in the Byzantine Age.

Page 173:
Wall mosaic depicting a ship in port. First or second century A.D. (Antiquario Communale, Rome.)

Page 174:
Ostia: Polychrome mosaic with representations of the months. Fourth century A.D.

APPENDICES

ROMAN MONUMENTS THROUGH THE AGES

From the time the city was founded up to the present, the site of Rome has always been inhabited, without any interruption whatever. It goes without saying that this has led to a continuous transformation of the urban texture and of individual buildings, a process in which it is difficult to perceive separate stages. The phenomenon was obviously to be observed even in ancient times; indeed it was rendered more acute by the frequent collapse of buildings, by fires, and by floods.

Nevertheless, the end of the ancient world marked a significant turning point. At that stage, the transformation not only became quantitatively larger, its character changed as well. The socioeconomic organization of the city in the early Middle Ages might be termed a return to a structure no longer urban and international, but sectorial, autarchical, and based on the village system. Among other things, this explains a fearful population drop. Although Rome remained, even during the Middle Ages, one of the principal cities of Europe, this was chiefly because of the presence of the papacy. The number of its actual inhabitants declined to the point that in 1377, when the popes returned from their exile in Avignon (the exile in fact marks the period of the city's greatest decadence), the population is said to have been no more than seventeen thousand. At that time a large part of the area within the Aurelian walls — perhaps more than three-quarters of it — was cultivated land, where the only constructions of any importance were churches and monasteries.

Because of these far-reaching social transformations, most of the buildings of Imperial Rome were naturally abandoned. They had been conceived for a city infinitely larger, the capital of a worldwide Empire. Rome was not only symbolic of that Empire but parasitic upon it, a city whose gigantic population could survive only by constant transfusions from the provinces, so the city's fall from its role as capital had immediate and grave effects. The fragile native economic structures of Rome and its hinterland could by no means support a structure of its expanded Imperial dimensions. The ancient monuments, then, were inevitably left to abandonment and decay when they could not somehow be pressed into use again, adapted to new functions. Virtually without exception, the best preserved buildings in Rome are precisely those for which new uses were promptly found. A typical example is the Pantheon, which was transformed into a Christian church as early as the seventh century A.D.

From abandonment to the next stage, the use of materials from the ancient monuments for new buildings, was a short step. A great many medieval buildings show clear signs of having been constructed in this way. Yet, all things considered, it must be said that the damage caused during this period was fairly light. At the end of the Middle Ages, ancient Rome was far better preserved than it is today. The most widespread destruction, customary opinion to the contrary, was caused precisely when interest in the ancient world was reawakened — during the Renaissance. The fact is that the population of the city increased tremendously at that time. Building activity inevitably increased as well and despite all protests and attempts at preservation, a large part of what remained of the ancient city was destroyed.

The result of these centuries of history is the character that the Roman monuments have gradually assumed. Integrated into structures of various epochs, adapted to the widest imaginable range of functions, they offer exceptional testimony to historical continuity. Buildings such as the Tabularium, on the Capitoline Hill, site of the public archives of the Roman state in the Republican era, then of the medieval Town Hall, and still in use today for the offices of the Rome's city administration, are in themselves sufficient to demonstrate the close historical connection between the different periods of the city's history.

The Change in Ground Level

Immediately visible to the naked eye, and a source of astonishment to all who visit the city, is the enormous difference between the ground level of the ancient monuments and that of the present day. It varies from place to place. There is a difference in level of perhaps seven feet at the square in front of the Pantheon; at the foot of the Quirinal, at the intersection of Via Quattro Fontane and Via Nazionale, the difference is some sixty feet. The phenomenon has taken place everywhere, of course. It resulted from the progressive accumulation of mud from floods and debris from dilapidated buildings that was left where it fell, from the building of terraces and other earthworks. Even in the ancient era there had been a rise in the level of the ground; the group of archaic monuments known as the *Lapis Niger*, in the Forum, is almost seven feet below the ground level of the Augustan Age. The process is of course much slower and less visible in periods of more intense life and more advanced civilization. In such periods paved streets are built and tend to remain in use over a long time, and they receive constant maintenance. In the periods of population decline and abandonment, on the other hand, the ground level rises rapidly. Waste materials accumulate, and, remaining where they lie, they are gradually shaped by natural processes (rain, winds, erosion, etc.) until new human settlements come into being above the old.

Even in places where life has gone on without interruption — as seems to have been the case in certain sections of the Campus Martius, where the modern quarters respect quite scrupulously the orientation and foundations of the old — an increase in the ground level can be observed, although it is usually less marked. A partial explanation is that construction of new buildings over those that have been demolished or have collapsed often utilized the walls remaining from the older buildings as a foundation. The phenomenon is widespread, as may be easily observed in visits to the cellars of Rome's historic areas.

From the Sack of Alaric to the Seventh Century

It is best to discuss the changes that have taken place in Rome's monuments by an account of the specific historic developments that have led to the present situation, although some of the episodes are known only in part. But one thing may be said: the legend that the destruction of Rome was caused by the invasions of the barbarians has long been deflated. The systematic destruction of imposing buildings — such as the Circus Maximus, very little of which has been preserved — was beyond both the will and capacities of those hordes, who usually remained in the city only a few days and confined themselves at most to the sacking of precious objects or, on occasions, to the burning of a building or two. The other traditional theory, which blames the destruction of pagan Rome on the Christians, is likewise based on no serious evidence. (Episodes such as the destruction of the Serapeum (Temple of Serapis) in Alexandria by the Christians in 391 were not common in Rome.) The only people who could in fact be considered responsible for the destruction of the ancient city are the inhabitants themselves. The process went on over a long period of time and virtually all the generations that have lived in the area of Rome have taken some part in it.

The process of demolition always went forward hand in hand with the reutilization of building materials; the city devoured itself only to come back into being in new forms. The custom of using parts of ancient monuments in new edifices was beginning to take hold even in the fourth century. The Villa and Circus of Maxentius and the Arch of Constantine, all noted earlier, are typical.

Alaric's sack of Rome in A.D. 410 was the first since the days of the Gallic fire exactly 800 years before. The damage caused was primarily to private homes; two letters written by Saint Gregory provide privileged contemporary testimony of the event. According to the archaeologist Rodolfo Lanciani, excavations carried out in the areas where the homes of patrician families were concentrated in a late period of the Empire, the Aventine and Coelian hills, have shown that the homes there were destroyed by a fire at the beginning of the fifth century and were not rebuilt. The home of Valerius Severus, prefect of Rome in A.D. 386, for example, was put up for sale in the year 404, but found no buyers. People seemed to be frightened by the imposing nature, and no doubt the equally imposing price of the building. A few years later, however, in 417, the house was sold at a very low price, because in the meantime it had been sacked and half-destroyed by the barbarians.

A number of public buildings on the Aventine — including what may have been the Decian Baths — were also damaged. In fact, an inscription records restorations carried out in the area in 414, four years after the sack. Many treasures were hidden at the time of the siege. Some were apparently not recovered before their owners died, and have been recovered in various epochs since. The most outstanding of these is "Proiecta's treasure," a large number of magnificent silver pieces, discovered on the Esquiline Hill (the bulk of them are now at the British Museum in London). An inscription noted that the treasure was the property of the wife of Turcius Asterius Secundus, prefect of the city in 362.

The ever-growing insecurity of the countryside after the fifth century resulted in the progressive abandonment of catacombs and the beginning of the custom, which later became quite normal, of burying the dead within the Aurelian walls. The sack of the Vandals in 455 caused a good deal of damage. The Temple of Jupiter Capitolinus and the Imperial palaces of the Palatine were sacked, among other things. Numerous statues were taken to Carthage, to decorate the home of King Genseric; a century later they were taken to Constantinople by Belisarius. The statues carried off as Roman booty during the Judaic war, and which Vespasian then had placed in the Forum of Peace, seem to have been among these.

With Theodoric (500–520) a certain recovery occurred. The Imperial palaces on the Palatine Hill were restored, as well as a number of other buildings, including the Theater of Pompey and the Colosseum. The principal documents showing that this activity was actually carried out are the letters sent by Cassiodorus to the city magistrates with instructions for the restoration and the preservation of the works of art. The numerous brick seals bearing the name of the king, as well as the inscriptions on the buildings themselves, faithfully confirm everything we know from the literary texts.

This was, however, the last flowering of artistic activity. It was followed almost immediately by a collapse. War broke out between the Byzantines and the Goths. The city was subjected to an uninterrupted series of sieges and destructive onslaughts and passed definitively into the Middle Ages. Among other things, Procopius records that the aqueducts destroyed during the siege of Vitige (537–538) were never later repaired. Although the waters of the aqueducts built underground

— such as the Aqua Virgo, the Appia, and the Anio Vetus — continued to flow into the city, from the sixth century on the great baths remained unused and were earmarked for certain destruction. Another result was the abandonment of the higher parts of the city, where the flow of water had stopped.

The description of the city Procopius gives in his book on the Gothic war shows that the larger part of the monuments and their decorations were still in good condition, but an episode in the war that took place around Hadrian's Tomb — even in the preceding century included as a front bulwark in the line of fortification — was an ill omen. The defenders, attacked by the Goths, who had camped in the vicinity of St. Peter's, repulsed the enemy forces by bombarding them with innumerable statues with which the building was still adorned.

The abandonment of the countryside surrounding the city, which was infested by brigands and malaria and overrun by hordes of the Longobards, characterized the end of the sixth century and the seventh century. Nevertheless, in the year 608 one last monument, the Column of Phocas, was erected in the Forum, set up by the prefect Smaragdus in honor of the Byzantine emperor who had donated the Pantheon to the Church. From that time on it became common to transform the pagan temples into churches, buildings that before this time Christians seem to have found repugnant.

In these same years the palaces on the Palatine Hill were evidently still in good condition, since Heraclius was crowned on the Palatine in 629, probably in the *Aula Regia* of the *Domus Flavia*. On this occasion the Emperor presented the Pope with the gilded bronze tiles that had covered the Temple of Venus and Roma, which were put to new use in St. Peter's. It is thus plain, according to Lanciani, that in this epoch the building must still have been well preserved.

Medieval Rome

The city in the ninth century is described in an itinerary drawn up for the use of pilgrims, known as "the Einsiedeln itinerary." Like all guidebooks worthy of the name, it is divided into itineraries that describe the monuments situated to the right and left of the roads to be followed. The roads correspond perfectly to those of the Imperial era; Carolingian Rome preserved, all in all, the city's original appearance. This itinerary may be compared with another dating from the end of the twelfth century, that of Benedict the Canon, and with the descriptions known as *Mirabilia*, or *Marvels of Rome*. The change was overwhelming. Besides the alterations that had taken place in the intervening years, a cultural upheaval had occurred as well. The ancient names of the buildings and streets have disappeared or are totally misrepresented, and the descriptions of the city, altogether fantastic, are interspersed with little moralizing fables typical of the Middle Ages. The Carolingian Age really represented the last attempt at recovering elements of classical culture that had remained accessible, though completely embalmed. Now even these scanty elements disappeared and were forgotten.

There were several key events in this period of more than three centuries. The Saracens attacked in 846, and although they did not conquer the city, they devastated the suburban quarters, sacking the treasures in St. Peter's and in St. Paul's basilica. The sack of the city by the Normans under Robert Guiscard in 1084 was even worse; of all the invasions of Rome, it was perhaps the most disastrous. The Campus Martius and the Coelian Hill were devastated. Traces of the event are to be found in the church of San Clemente, which was half-destroyed to the extent that it was rebuilt on a level more than ten feet higher. Today this venerable building, with its three superimposed levels (the building of Roman days, with a Mithreum [Temple of Mithras], the primitive church, and the church of the twelfth century) constitutes the most striking synthesis of twenty centuries of Roman history.

In this period the major monuments were occupied and adapted to functions completely different from those for which they were built. As a rule they became fortifications for the use of the more powerful Roman families. The Frangipani family occupied the Colosseum and a large part of the Palatine Hill. The Savellis fortified themselves in the Theater of Marcellus, the Orsinis in the Theater of Pompey, the Colonnas in the Forum of Trajan and the Temple of Serapis on the Quirinal. The tomb of Cecilia Metella became a tower in the castle of the Caetanis. At this time Rome — not unlike the other principal cities of Central Italy — must have looked like a series of small fortified villages, with towers rising high above their roofs. The Tor de'Conti, mentioned by Dante and Petrarch as the highest tower in existence at the time — it collapsed in 1348 — was built at Rome, in an exedra of the Forum of Peace.

Export and Destruction in the Late Middle Ages

It was in the twelfth century, at the outset of the "Romanesque Renaissance," that the sacking of the ancient monuments began on a wide scale. In this phase, the emphasis was not so much on buildings as on decorative marbles, capitals, stone or marble slabs, and inscriptions, which were used primarily for the decoration of new buildings. Anyone even superficially familiar with the churches of Rome knows how frequently their builders resorted to pilfered ancient materials, particularly columns, capitals, and inscriptions. The workshops of the marble carvers who were then intensely active (especially the Cosmati and Vassalletto families) renewed a large number of Rome's sacred buildings in those years, making abundant use of ancient marbles and stones. Lanciani estimates that in the floor of a minor church, such as that of the Quattro Santi Coronati, some two hundred inscriptions were used and not less than a thousand on St. Paul's Outside the Walls.

Nor was the custom confined to Rome. Export flourished, and was usually handled as cheaply as possible, by sea. It had begun as early as the reign of Theodoric, who had the columns of the Imperial residence on the Pincian hill taken to Ravenna. The same thing happened in the Carolingian era at Aix-la-Chapelle, where marbles from Rome were used in local buildings. Exportation reached its peak, however, in the closing centuries of the Middle Ages. Materials from Rome and Ostia were used in the Cathedral of Pisa, begun in 1063. To all appearances there were shipped to the Tuscan town by sea. There is an inscription dedicated to the "Genius" of the Colony of Ostia in the cathedral, and many of the sarcophagi in the Pisa Cemetery were no doubt brought in from the same place. The same process occurred later on in the cathedral of Orvieto, as contemporary documents mention. The materials used there had been purloined from the Tomb of Hadrian, the Portico of Octavia, the Temple of Isis in the Campus Martius and, outside Rome, from Veii and Domitian's villa near Lake Albano.

Another cause of destruction, less apparent but more lethal, was the setting up of numerous *calcare*, stone-grinding and stone-baking plants that transformed into lime whatever was not judged suitable for further use. In this manner entire monumental buildings of travertine or marble disappeared. The kilns were scattered all over the city (one was even found inside the tomb of the Scipios), but the most important were in the Campus Martius, in the area where Via delle Botteghe Oscure and Largo Argentina are now located. Sixteenth century maps show the terrible workshops, still in operation. The place names of the area bore signs of this activity for a long time. S. Nicola de Calcarario, which occupied the space of Temple A of the Largo Argentina, has now disappeared. There were also SS. Quaranta de Calcarario and Santa Lucia de Calcarario. Excavations in the sacred area of the Largo Argentina have brought to light a remarkable number of marble fragments — sculptures, foundation stones, inscriptions — which undoubtedly came from the monuments, or even the tombs, of the surrounding area. Without question, they were gathered here to be made into lime. Monument after monument of Republican and Imperial Rome was devoured by the kilns.

The Depredations of the Renaissance

During the period that saw the transference of the papacy to Avignon (1309–1377), very little building went on in Rome, and it is unlikely that the ancient monuments suffered much harm. One of the rare works of importance carried out in this period was the great stairway of Santa Maria in Aracoeli, whose 124 steps were taken from the Temple of Serapis on the Quirinal.

The situation changed radically in the centuries that followed. For Rome the Renaissance represents a period of widespread recovery. Under the impetus of popes like Sixtus IV, Julius II, and Leo X, public works were undertaken on an impressive scale and the urban structure of the city was revolutioned. As is always the case, the intense building activity caused considerable destruction. The new city spread into areas already occupied by ancient quarters; builders continued to make use of materials from ancient buildings for their new constructions. The destruction continued undisturbed, despite the reawakened interest in the classical world that marked Renaissance culture, and even the protests of cultivated people were of no avail. In Lanciani's history of excavations there are a great many documents on the subject. Particularly impressive is the number of "digging permits" issued to entrepreneurs who then had a free hand in demolishing ancient structures to recover building materials.

A list of the monuments that disappeared in this way would be very long. It is sufficient to mention the destruction under Sixtus IV of a circular Temple of Hercules and two arches of the Augustan Age in the Forum Boarium; the demolition of a grandiose monumental sepulcher in the form of a pyramid, similar to that of Gaius Cestius (the so-called *Meta Romuli*), of part of the Baths of Diocletian, and the Forum Transitorium under Alexander VI; the almost total destruction of the Temple of Venus and Roma and the Arch of Gratian, Valentinian, and Theodosius under Nicholas V; and the destruction of the *Septizodium* under Sixtus V. In 1452 alone one entrepreneur, a certain Giovanni Paglia, a Lombard, took no less than 2,522 cart loads of travertine from the Colosseum in nine months. The depredation of the Colosseum continued unabated. Material from it was used, among other things, to build the Palazzo della Cancellaria.

In some cases the destruction was averted by a miracle. A letter written by the architect Domenico Fontana to his master, Sixtus V, dated January 4, 1588, requests permission to destroy the Arch of the Argentari in order to use its materials for the foundation of an obelisk that had been taken from the Circus Maximus and was to be set up near St. John Lateran. Fortunately the foundation was built later with other marble and the Arch was saved. The pontificate of Sixtus V was one of the most disastrous for the ancient monuments. Besides the *Septizodium*, which Fontana demolished in the years 1588–1589 (the business-like architect even noted the expense: 905 scudi), the Baths of Diocletian suffered greatly (about 3,200,000 square yards of brickwork were, it seems, removed) as did the Claudian aqueduct. Even medieval buildings were demolished, including the *Patriarchium* of the Lateran, the ancient Papal See, by all accounts the most important building in medieval Rome. Meanwhile, the sculptor Flaminio Vacca, writing of the discoveries made in Rome during his lifetime, mentions that the capitals of the Temple of Jupiter Capitolinus, which were uncovered in the sixteenth century, were reused, among other things, for the statues carved for the Cesi Chapel in the Church of Santa Maria del Populo.

The Monuments Since the Eighteenth Century

Renaissance interest in ancient art was the direct cause of destruction to many of the monuments. To recover statues and other objets d'art for the collections of popes, princes, and cardinals, excavations were made which considerably damaged the ancient buildings. Nor did the ensuing centuries alter the rather cavalier attitude taken toward the city's heritage. A radical turning point was reached only in the eighteenth century, with the rise of a scientific archaeology. It was then that Winckelmann established guidelines for the study of the history of ancient art, and excavations were begun at Herculaneum and Pompeii. At the beginning of the nineteenth century two great abutments were erected to support the tottering walls of the Colosseum, and the systematic pillaging of the buildings was brought to an end. At the same time scientific excavations were begun in Rome — those of the Forum were of particular importance — and archaeological and topographical studies reached an exceptionally high level with scholars such as Visconti, Fea, Nibby, and Canina.

One episode, however, shows how wide a gap still existed between the attitude of the conservators and scholars and that of the contemporary society. In 1870 Piux IX ordered the demolition of the Porta Tiburtina, which had been rebuilt by Honorius. The Pope intended to reuse the materials for a column he wished to have erected in front of the Church of S. Pietro in Montorio, but the work was brusquely interrupted by the entry of Italian troops into Rome.

In the history of the ancient monuments during the last one hundred years, three distinct phases can be distinguished: the period from 1870 to the end of the First World War; the period of Fascism; and the years following the the Second World War. One characteristic is common to all: the indiscriminate expansion of the city, which never succeeded in providing itself with an effective modern town-plan. From the standpoint of safeguarding the monuments, the first period was perhaps the least disastrous. Soon after the capture of Rome by the troops of United Italy (1870), the Commissione Archeologica Communale was established. It carried out meritorious projects of conservation and study of the artifacts and remains that creation of new sections of the city kept bringing to light — primarily on the Quirinal and the Esquiline.

The twenty-year period of Fascism was ruinous. An enormous amount of lip service was paid to the importance of Roman antiquities, but they were exploited for political ends and in reality were subjected to heavy treatment. Two examples among many were the pointless demolition of the *Meta sudante*, the grandiose fountain near the Colosseum, and the building of the Via dell'Impero, which not only covered, or rather swallowed, an entire hill of ancient Rome, the Velian, as well as other ancient sections, but did not even bring the Imperial Forums to light. In fact the area of the Forums now visible is no larger than that visible before the change was made. Areas uncovered were reburied in such great haste under the gigantic avenue that at times archaeologists were not given a chance to carry out their investigations with care.

The Fascist period was characterized in actuality by a total lack of respect for the ancient monuments as historical documents. They were instead "isolated" and "evaluated" in connection with well-defined practical objectives, and then exploited as an expression of "new values." This reinterpretation of antiquities for political reasons was obvious in cases like the isolation of the Capitoline Hill, which led to the destruction of entire medieval and Renaissance sections, among the most beautiful in all Rome, and the "liberation" of the Mausoleum of Augustus, which not only caused similar damage but "endowed" the center of the city with one of its most repellent piazzas. That the "esthetic" vision behind these measures had political and practical, rather than a truly historical or scientific basis, was made most clear by the demolition of brick buildings of the Imperial Age, which occupied the presently empty spaces between the Republican temples of the Largo Argentina; their columns now remain, isolated, like a fine rhetorical gesture, in an absolute vacuum. The projects that were not carried out were perhaps even more ambitious. Among other things, it was proposed to isolate the Theater of Pompey, by lengthening the Corso Rinascimento as far as the Ponte Sisto. Then the war came, and defeat put a stop to the work. For a regime that considered the exaltation of ancient Roman virtues one of its chief goals, the performances of the Fascist period were awfully poor.

Although the postwar period brought an awareness of historical and environmental values much less barbaric than during the preceding period, it brought its own scourge: building speculation. Since the day Rome was proclaimed the Italian capital, such speculation had been on the rise, but it reached its greatest heights after the Second World War. The Umbertian and Fascist periods were responsible for the massacre of much of Rome's historical center; the present period will go down in history as that which brought about the total destruction of the suburban area. The great consular roads and the monuments that surrounded them — tombs, villas, and aqueducts, not to mention the landscape and countryside — were systematically destroyed. Only a few fragments have survived this colossal "prosperity." After the true monuments had been destroyed, an effort was made to create imitations. In this "Romanization of the periphery" operation, municipal warehouses were emptied of architraves and columns, which were placed on traffic islands in the various suburban neighborhoods. Could it be that, in such a development, we find ourselves arriving at the crossroads with a historical constant: a refined historical-critical conscience on the part of a cultured elite always goes hand in hand with a period of ever-greater destruction and desecration? But that is another subject to explore in a different book. For now, we can only conclude that we must all be wary of the many forces at work if we are to preserve the best monuments and finer elements of the civilization of ancient Rome.

CHRONOLOGICAL CHART
OF ROMAN HISTORY

DATE	MONUMENTS	HISTORICAL EVENTS
800 B.C.	Remains of huts from the Iron Age on the Palatine The Forum Necropolis.	753 B.C. Traditional date of the founding of Rome.
750 B.C.		750 B.C. (circa) Foundation of Cumae, the first Greek colony in the west.
700 B.C.	Great tombs of eastern type at Cerveteri and Praeneste.	The first legendary kings of Rome: Romulus, Numa Pompilius, Tullus Hostilius, Ancus Martius.
650 B.C.	Construction of the first bridge over the Tiber (the Sublicius), traditionally attributed to Ancus Martius.	616 B.C. Legendary arrival of Tarquinius Priscus in Rome. Beginning of Etruscan domination through Etruscan kings in Rome: 616–579 B.C. Tarquinius Priscus.
600 B.C.	First installation of the Circus Maximus.	579–534 B.C. Servius Tullius, King of Rome.
550 B.C.	Temple of Diana on the Aventine and Temples of Fortuna and of Mater Matuta in Forum Boarium, founded by Servius Tullius. First "Servian Wall" (?) Cloaca Maxima, constructed during reign of Tarquinius Superbus 509 B.C. Inauguration of Temple of Jupiter Capitolinus.	534–509 B.C. Tarquinius Superbus, King of Rome. 509 B.C. End of the monarchical period; beginning of the Republic.
500 B.C.	493 B.C. Temple of Ceres, Liber, and Libera inaugurated, the work of Greek artists.	
450 B.C.	431 B.C. Temple of Apollo inaugurated.	
400 B.C.	378 B.C. Reconstruction of "Servian" wall.	396 B.C. Roman conquest of Veii, the major Etruscan city nearest Rome. 390 B.C. Conquest and sack of Rome by the Gauls.
350 B.C.	Temple C in the Largo Argentina. 312 B.C. Appian Way, from Rome to Capua. 304–303 B.C. Fabius the Painter paints the Temple of Salus. Francois Tomb at Vulci (named for its 19th-century discoverer).	343–341 B.C. First Samnite War. 326–304 B.C. Second Samnite War, for the domination of Campania.
300 B.C.	270 B.C. (circa) Italic temple at Paestum. Sepulcher of the Scipios (on the Appian Way).	298–290 B.C. Third Samnite War. 281–272 B.C. War against Tarentum and Pyrrhus.
250 B.C.		264–241 B.C. First Punic War, with Carthage over possession of Sicily. 218–202 B.C. Second Punic War, against Hannibal and Carthage. 211 B.C. Conquest of Syracuse, ally of the Carthaginians. 209 B.C. Conquest of Tarentum, which had been occupied by Hannibal.
200 B.C.	190 B.C. (circa) Arrival of first Hellenistic artists from Asia Minor. 180–145 B.C. Activity of first Attic artists for Roman patrons. After 177 B.C. Luni pottery and ceramics.	190 B.C. Battle of Magnesia against Antiochus III of Syria.

150 B.C.	"House of the Faun" at Pompeii. First phase (?) of the "Villa of Mysteries," Pompeii. 146–102 B.C. Activity of Greek architect Hermodorus of Salamis in Rome. Circular temple in Forum Boarium. Temple of Fortuna at Praeneste. "House of the Griffins" in Rome.	146 B.C. Destruction of Corinth and Carthage, in the Third Punic War. 102–101 B.C. Marius defeats the Cimbri and the Teutons.
100 B.C.	*Ara* of Domitius Enobarbus. 80–78 B.C. Construction of *Tabularium*, Roman state archives on the Capitol. Temple of Hercules at Tivoli. Temple of Jupiter Anxur at Terracina. Little Theater and Amphitheater at Pompeii. 55 B.C. Inauguration of Theater of Pompey in Rome.	91–88 B.C. Social War, against Italic allies claiming citizenship. 88–82 B.C. Civil War, between Marius and Sulla, won by Sulla.
50 B.C.	54–46 B.C. Forum of Caesar Beginning of Aretine ceramic production. 40–30 B.C. Tomb of Eurysaces (Tomb of the Baker), in Rome near the Porta Maggiore. 9 B.C. Inauguration of *Ara Pacis* 2 B.C. Inauguration of Forum of Augustus Villa at Sperlonga. Villa at Capri.	48 B.C. Death of Pompey. 44 B.C. Death of Julius Caesar. 31 B.C. Battle of Actium, between Octavius and Antony, allied with Cleopatra, Queen of Egypt, for the control of power in Rome.
B.C. **0** **A.D.**		Julian-Claudian Emperors: 23 B.C.–A.D. 14 Augustus A.D. 15–37 Tiberius. A.D. 37–41 Caligula. A.D. 41–54 Claudius. A.D. 54–68 Nero.
A.D. 50	A.D. 64 Construction of *Domus Aurea;* Severus and Celer, architects. A.D. 80 Colosseum (Flavian Amphitheater). Arch of Titus. Baths of Titus. Palace of Domitian on the Palatine; Rabirius, architect. Forum of Nerva.	A.D. 64 Fire in Rome. A.D. 69 Emperors Galba, Otho, and Vitellius. Flavian Emperors: A.D. 69–79 Vespasian. A.D. 79–82 Titus A.D. 82–96 Domitian. A.D. 96–98 Nerva. A.D. 98–117 Trajan.
A.D. 100	A.D. 112–113 Inauguration of Forum of Trajan and Column of Trajan; reconstruction of Forum of Caesar. A.D. 118–128 The Pantheon. A.D. 125–135 Hadrian's Villa.	Antonine Emperors: A.D. 117–138 Hadrian. A.D. 138–161 Antoninus Pius.
A.D. 150	Temple of Divine Hadrian. Sepulchers in Via Latina. *Pago Triopio*, the villa of Herod Atticus on Appian Way. Column of Marcus Aurelius. A.D. 196 Restoration of the theater at Ostia.	A.D. 161–180 Marcus Aurelius. A.D. 180–193 Commodus.
A.D. 200	A.D. 203 Arch of Septimius Severus. A.D. 204 Arch of the Argentari. A.D. 212–216 Baths of Caracalla.	Severian Emperors: A.D. 193–211 Septimius Severus. A.D. 211–217 Caracalla. A.D. 217–218 Macrinus. A.D. 218–222 Heliogabalus A.D. 222–235 Alexander Severus.
A.D. 250	A.D. 270–274 Construction of the Aurelian Walls. A.D. 298–306 Palace of Diocletian at Spalato.	A.D. 235–284 Period of military anarchy: twenty-one emperors. A.D. 284–305 Diocletian Tetrarchy: division of the Empire into four districts, each with its own emperor.
A.D. 300	A.D. 303 Base of the Diocletian Decennial monument in the Forum. Circus and Villa of Maxentius. Temple of Romulus in the Forum. Reconstruction of Temple of Venus and Roma. Basilica of Maxentius. A.D. 312–315 Arch of Constantine. Four-faced Arch of the Forum Boarium. Mausoleum of Constantina (Santa Costanza).	A.D. 306–337 Constantine. A.D. 312 Battle of Milvian Bridge between Constantine and Maxentius for domination of Italy. A.D. 313 Edict of Milan, granting freedom of worship to Christians. A.D. 330 Inauguration of Constantinople.
A.D. 400		A.D. 410 Sack of Rome by Alaric. A.D. 476 Fall of western Roman Empire; Emperor Romulus Augustus deposed by Odoacer, King of Herulians.

RECOMMENDED READING

There is almost no end to the books about the ancient Romans; the problem is to find those suited to a reader's particular needs. This list is a representative selection of books that might well complement various aspects of this volume. They have also been chosen on the basis of their accessibility — price, recent printings, and attempts to communicate with the general public.

Ashby, Thomas: *The Roman Campagna in Classical Times* (Barnes & Noble, 1971)

Bloch, Raymond: *The Origins of Rome* (Praeger, 1960)

Brown, Frank: *Roman Architecture* (Braziller, 1961)

Carcopino, Jerome: *Daily Life in Ancient Rome* (Yale Univ. Press, 1940)

Davenport, Basil, ed.: *The Portable Roman Reader* (Viking, 1951)

Dudley, Donald: *The Civilization of Rome* (New American Library, 1960)
   Urbs Roma: A Source Book of Classical Texts on the City and Its Monuments (Phaidon 1967)

Grant, Michael: *The Roman Forum* (Macmillan, 1970)
   The World of Rome (Praeger, 1970)

Grimal, Pierre: *In Search of Ancient Italy* (Hill & Wang, 1964)

Hadas, Moses, ed.: *The History of Rome from Its Origins to AD 529 as Told by the Roman Historians* (Doubleday, 1956)

Hafner, German: *The Art of Rome, Etruria, and Magna Graecia* (Abrams, 1970)

Hanfmann, George M.: *Roman Art: A Modern Survey of the Art of Imperial Rome* (N.Y. Graphic Society, 1964)

Lissner, Ivan: *The Caesars* (Putnam, 1958)

Livy: *The Early History of Rome* (Penguin, 1960)

Paoli, Ugo: *Rome: Its People, Life and Customs* (McKay, 1963)

Petrie, Alexander: *Introduction to Roman History, Literature, and Antiquities* (Oxford Univ. Press, 1963)

Picard, Gilbert: *Living Architecture: Rome* (Grosset & Dunlap, 1970)

Plutarch: *Lives of the Noble Romans* (Various editions)

Starr, Chester: *The Civilization of the Caesars* (Norton, 1965)

Stenico, Arturo: *Roman and Etruscan Painting* (Viking, 1963)

Suetonius: *Lives of the Twelve Caesars* (Various editions)

Von Hagen, Victor: *Roman Roads* (World, 1966)

Wheeler, Mortimer: *Roman Art and Architecture* (Praeger, 1966)

RECOMMENDED VIEWING

Nothing quite compares with visiting the actual sites of the Romans or the great collections of their art and artifacts in the museums of Italy; the modern age of jet travel and tourism makes this relatively easy. The next best thing is a visit to a museum with a collection of Roman antiquities, and there are many such major collections in Great Britain and North America. The most important are:

    Ashmolean Museum, Oxford
    Birmingham City Museum and Art Gallery, Birmingham
    The British Museum, London
    Fitzwilliam Museum, Cambridge
    Laing Art Gallery and Museum, Newcastle upon Tyne
    The Metropolitan Museum of Art, New York City
    The Museum of Fine Arts, Boston, Massachusetts
    The University Museum, Univ. of Pennsylvania, Philadelphia
    The Cleveland Museum of Art, Ohio
    The Rhode Island School of Design Museum of Art, Providence
    The Victoria and Albert Museum, London

Listed below are the many other collections—all open, with certain restrictions, to the general public—that offer people throughout North America, a chance to make at least some acquaintance with Roman remains.

Alabama: Birmingham Museum of Art
California: Berkeley: Pacific School of Religion, Palestine Institute Museum
    Los Angeles County Museum of Art
    Malibu: J. Paul Getty Museum
    Santa Barbara Museum of Art
Colorado: Denver Art Museum
Connecticut: Hartford: Wadsworth Atheneum
    New Haven: Yale University Art Gallery
Hawaii: Honolulu Academy of Arts
Illinois: Urbana: University of Illinois Cultural Museum
Indiana: Bloomington: Indiana University Museum of Art
Kansas: Lawrence: University of Kansas, Wilcox Museum
Maine: Brunswick: Bowdoin College Museum of Art
Maryland: Baltimore: Johns Hopkins University, Archaeological Museum
    The Walters Art Gallery
Massachusetts: Cambridge: Harvard University, Fogg Art Museum
    Northampton: Smith College Museum of Art
    Provincetown: Chrysler Art Museum
    Worcester Art Museum
Michigan: Ann Arbor: University of Michigan, Kelsey Museum of Archaeology
    Detroit Institute of the Arts
Minnesota: Minneapolis Art Institute
Missouri: Columbus: University of Missouri, Museum of Art and Archaeology
    Kansas City: William R. Nelson Gallery & Atkins Museum of Fine Arts
    St. Louis Art Museum
New Jersey: The Newark Museum
    Princeton University Art Museum
New York: Albany Institute of History and Art
    New York City: Brooklyn Museum
    Rochester: Memorial Gallery, University of Rochester
North Carolina: Raleigh: North Carolina Museum of Art
Ohio: Cincinnati Art Museum
    Dayton Art Institute
    Toledo Museum of Art
Oregon: Portland Art Museum
Texas: Houston: Museum of Fine Arts
Washington: Seattle Art Museum
Washington, D.C : The Dumbarton Oaks Research Library and Collection
Wisconsin: Milwaukee Public Museum
    Milwaukee: Charles Allis Art Library
Canada: Montreal Museum of Fine Arts
    Toronto: Royal Ontario Museum, University of Toronto

INDEX